# The Obscure and Fun Facts of the Faroe Islands

*A Travel Guide and Alternative Introduction to Faroese Society and Culture*

Written by:
## Rúni í Múla

The information provided in this book is for entertainment purposes only and may be outdated on specific prices, opening hours and contact information for the different places. The author and publisher of this book make no representations or warranties of any kind, express or implied, about the completeness, accuracy, reliability, suitability or availability with respect to the information, products, services, or related graphics contained in this book for any purpose. Any reliance you place on such information is, therefore, strictly at your own risk.

**COPYRIGHT © 2023 BY RÚNI Í MÚLA**
The Obscure and Fun Facts of the Faroe Islands: A Travel Guide and Alternative Introduction to Faroese Society and Culture

**Notice of Copyright**

This book is copyright protected by the author. No part of this book may be reproduced, stored in a retrieval system, or transmitted in any form or by any means, electronic, mechanical, photocopying, recording, or otherwise, without the prior written permission of the author. This book is for personal use only and may not be resold or given away to other people.

**ISBN**: 9798392097807

**Self-published by author**

**First Printed Edition, 2023**

RÚNI Í MÚLA

*Map of the Faroe Islands*

THE OBSCURE AND FUN FACTS OF THE FAROE ISLANDS

# Table of Contents

Preface ................................................................. ix
Introduction ........................................................... 1
   Denmark, not Denmark ................................... 3
   Operation Valentine ......................................... 9
   The Death Penalty ......................................... 17
   Religion and Superstition ............................... 25
   The Language and the Nobel Prize ............... 31
   Cartology and the Faroes .............................. 37
   Animal Life ................................................... 43
   Challenging Delicacies................................... 57
   Faroese Currencies....................................... 63
   Vehicles and Vessels.................................... 69
   Cinematography and Movies ........................ 77
   Public Service and Bingo.............................. 83
   World Records.............................................. 89
   Fun Facts ..................................................... 99

The Unique Travel Guide................................... 129
   Art, Music and Culture................................ 131
   History and Historic Sites ........................... 141
   Restaurants and Dining .............................. 155

Distilleries and Breweries ............................................. 163
Well-known Gems in Nature ........................................ 175
Hidden Gems in Nature ................................................ 183
Exclusive and Authentic High-end Souvenirs ............. 205
How to get around ......................................................... 209
Safety Guidelines for Driving ...................................... 217
Safety Guidelines for Hiking ........................................ 219
Important Websites ...................................................... 223
Important Phone Numbers .......................................... 225

# Preface

This book is made as an effort for a new and more interesting take on a traditional travel guidebook, with many interesting stories, facts and places worth visiting. To me, visitors seem to always see and visit the same places and are mostly presented with the same stories. With this book, I have tried my best to provide you with all that isn't presented normally, so that you might have the best experience while visiting the Faroe Islands. This has been my motivation for making this book.

The book is structured in two main parts. One is about fun and fascinating facts about the Faroes. At the same time, the second is a unique travel guide, where many places are highlighted that aren't usually accessible to tourists, but also inducing some of the most visited places worth visiting. Also, in this section, I have highlighted some of the best things to do during your stay and a list of important phone numbers and contact information, including some safety guidelines that will help you during your stay.

If you read the book out of pure interest, the book's first part is for you. If you plan on travelling to the Faroes, the first part can serve as a cultural introduction, while the second will serve as the travel guide that will give you the best experience you can have while staying. Know, however, that if you decide to discuss some of this book's contents with locals, chances are, that they haven't heard about many of the fascinating facts and stories contained within these pages.

Wishing you a pleasant reading and a great stay in the Faroe Islands, should you decide to go.

*Rúni í Múla*

*May 2023, Kunoy*

# THE OBSCURE AND FUN FACTS OF THE FAROE ISLANDS

*A Travel Guide and Alternative Introduction to Faroese Society and Culture*

# Introduction

North of Scotland, between Iceland and Norway, in the rushing North Atlantic Ocean, there is a small isolated archipelago with high mountains and harsh nature. These are the Faroe Islands - one of the world's smallest nations.

The archipelago comprises 18 small islands distinguished by steep cliffs, tall mountains, narrow fjords, and a population of some 50,000 people.

The Faroese language is descended from Old Norse, the language spoken by the Norsemen who settled the islands 1200 years ago.

The Faroese have defied harsh nature and living conditions for centuries. Today, it is a nation with one of the highest living standards in the world. A highly industrial economy based primarily on fisheries and aquaculture thrives, while a Nordic welfare model ensures everyone can realise their full potential. The Faroe Islands are well-known for their maritime expertise and export seafood to all six continents.

The Faroe Islands are strategically located between Europe and North America and are only a few hours flight from major cities in Northern Europe. The scenery upon arrival provides visitors with a captivating natural experience in a society with advanced infrastructure and digital networks.

Centuries of relative isolation have resulted in the preservation of ancient traditions that shape life in the Faroe Islands to this day. The Faroese society is distinguished by its unique blend of traditional and modern culture, which fosters a strong sense of local community and an active outlook as a globalised Nordic nation.

With this book, you will get an alternative introduction to the Faroese society with all the strange, interesting and obscure facts and fascinating insights about life on the islands, which you won't find in any other history- or guidebook. Additionally, this book contains recommendations for all the must-sees and does if you decide to visit the islands.

I hope you'll enjoy reading it and that this book might serve as a conversation starter should you decide to visit the Faroe Islands.

# Denmark, not Denmark

## The Political Status of the Faroe Islands

In the Færeyinga saga, the Story of the Faroe Islanders, it is said that the first Viking settlers were Norwegian emigrants who, because of high taxes, sought to Iceland. On their way, they came to the Faroe Islands, and some of the Norwegians decided to stay there. The Færeyinga saga tells of the famous folk hero, Sigmundur Brestisson, who brought Christianity to the islands around the year 1.000 and did so in the service of the Norwegian king, Harald Hairfair. Since then, the Faroe Islands became part of the Kingdom of Norway and stayed under Norwegian rule until 1814. Norway entered the Kalmar Union in 1397, and during that union, Norway eventually came under Danish control and remained in the Kingdom of Denmark until the Treaty of Kiel in 1814. When Norway gained sovereignty, the Faroe Islands, Iceland and Greenland continued within the Danish kingdom.

Today, the Faroe Islands have become a self-ruling territory, which might be hard to understand from an outsider's perspective because if it's not a sovereign state and not a

*The Faroese flag, Merkið, and the Danish flag, Dannebrog*

Danish county, then what is it? In geopolitics, this often becomes evident when the Faroe Islands try to become part of international associations because the state definitions do seldom fit the reality of the Denmark/Faroe relationship.

## The Danish Constitution

The Constitutional Act of the Kingdom of Denmark (Danmarks Riges Grundlov) is the Constitution of the Danish Kingdom of Realm. It is one of the oldest constitutions in the world and was first adopted in 1849 and has since been replaced with newer revisions. The latest revised version is from 1953, explicitly mentioning the Faroe Islands and Greenland in several articles.

Faroese politicians have often discussed whether the Faroe Islands ever adopted the Constitution and whether the Faroe Islands should recognise the Constitution. These politicians are typically on the nationalist political wing, while most non-nationalists recognise it. But politicians across all the political spectre have also asked whether the Constitution represents the actual relationship between Denmark and the Faroe Islands, many of whom argue that the Constitution in several areas has been outdated from the political practices and agreements that exist between the two nations. Some have also argued that the Home Rule Act is against the Constitution. The Constitution is nonetheless the binding legislation in which the Faroese self-rule via the Home Rule Act is granted.

## Independence or Home Rule?

During the Second World War, the Faroe Islands had been under British administration, and during those years, the ties to Denmark had been completely cut off. When the war settled, and Denmark was free from German occupation, the future of the relationship between Denmark and the Faroe Islands was uncertain. Denmark proposed a Home Rule Act similar to Iceland before they voted for independence. Still, the Faroese parliament wouldn't recognise this new Danish law, even though it meant the Faroe Islands would gain self-governance. Therefore, an independence referendum was decided where the citizens could choose between two options. The choices were:

1. To adopt the Home Rule Act
2. To get independence from Denmark

Two political parties were against the vote because they wanted more options. Therefore the People's Party asked their supporters to write "no" beside option one and to vote for option two, while the Social Democrats advised their voters to do the same thing, only the opposite. The referendum participation was 67,5 %, of which 4,1 % of the votes were deemed invalid. The final result was 50,7 % for independence and 49,3 % for home rule. In that way, the referendum's result was a slight yes for independence. Still, because the results were so close and because of the low participation rate, the

Danish officials did not recognise the result, stating that such decisions with such fundamental changes should have a more apparent result.

So the vote for independence was not recognised, and instead, the Faroe Islands got its Home Rule Act, giving the islands an extended self-governance. This law contained two lists, list A and list B, where certain political areas were highlighted that the Faroe Islands could gain complete control over without any political discussions with the Danish authorities (list A) and areas which could be overtaken through political negotiations (list B).

By 2005 most of the listed areas had been overtaken, and therefore the Home Rule was extended by two additional laws which expanded the Faroese autonomy regarding fisheries and international affairs.

THE OBSCURE AND FUN FACTS OF THE FAROE ISLANDS

# Operation Valentine

## The British Occupation during World War II

From the 12th of April 1940 to the 10th of June 1942, the British Military occupied the Faroe Islands under an operation called *Operation Valentine*. This was just after the German invasion of Denmark and Norway on the 9th of April 1940, which occurred only three days before. On the day before the German invasion, Winston Churchill said that the British army had discussed the North Atlantic situation and decided to occupy the Faroe Islands. On the 12th of April, two officers came on land in Tórshavn and announced their visit and the day after, 250 soldiers arrived at a foreign country, many of them believed to be Norway.

The British occupation proved to play a crucial role when it came to the development of the Faroese society. It was the British Military who made the first airport, and they also built roads in many places where no roads had been before. They brought the cinema with them and taught the Faroese people modern dance, which is still called *Eingilskur dansur,* English dance. Sweets and chocolate were also first introduced, and to

*Picture from the fort in Nes, Eysturoy*

this day, you can still buy English brands such as Dairymilk and Digestive biscuits, even though most of the imported goods on the Faroe Islands come from Denmark.

During the occupation, the Faroese society saw a transformation which had never been seen before. At times, as many as 8.000 British soldiers were on the islands and during their stay, many Faroese / British marriages took place, and many children were born.

## Faroe or Pharaoh?

When the war started, and men were sent to the Faroe Islands, some soldiers ended up in Egypt. Because of the name Faroe, British military officials thought they meant Egypt, mistaking the Faroes for the Pharaohs.

A young graduate who had just finished his studies in Middle-Eastern Studies was interviewed for a position in the British Intelligence Forces; at the interview, he was asked what his credentials were. He told them he spoke and wrote Arabic and could also read hieroglyphics. The interviewer then asked him what hieroglyphics were, and he replied that it was the written language of the pharaohs. The young scholar was therefore sent to the Faroe Islands.

## Fights over Women

The British soldiers were very well integrated into the Faroese society during the occupation. They were living amongst the locals throughout the country, and there were many British-Faroese marriages during this time. Many children were born, which explains the many different English last names still found today.

Compared to the average Faroese man, the British soldiers were well-dressed in their uniforms. They could dance and play instruments and were said to be very well-mannered. They did not share the same drinking habits as the Faroese, many of whom were binge drinkers.

This made the Englishmen much more desirable to many of the young women of the time than the average Faroese man. And this was also something that the Faroese men noticed, which often led to a fight or two, especially during the dances held on weekends.

Often, when dances were held in the local theatre in Tórshavn, the British soldiers would only allow Faroese women to come inside. In contrast, the men weren't allowed to enter but had to wait outside, and had they been angry with the soldiers beforehand, this didn't make the situation any better. Especially outside this theatre, many quarrels were between the men from Tórshavn and the British soldiers, and similar stories have also been told in Vágar.

## Faroeitis

Soldiers who had fought in close combat in battles in Europe and who had escaped without any physical harm were sometimes stationed in the Faroe Islands during the occupation. These were traumatised soldiers who had experienced high stress on the battlefields of the European mainland who were now in a place where no battles were fought and where there seemingly was no danger other than the air strikes and the mines floating in the sea around the archipelago.

While the British soldiers who were stationed on the island of Vágar had to be hardworking as they were building a primary base for the military, constructing roads, and even building an airfield situated at the same place where the modern airport is today, many of the soldiers who were stationed at other locations on the islands had close to nothing to do and were caught in severe boredom.

Then, a British military doctor noticed the condition he would later call *Faroeitis*.

The signs of Faroeitis started with the soldiers becoming depressed because of the high stress they had had in their battles in Europe, combined with the boredom they were experiencing now that they had no daily routines and were free of any danger. The second stage of the condition was the soldiers reporting that the sheep had started speaking with them. In this condition's third and final stage, the soldiers began talking back to the sheep.

Faroeitis, some then concluded, was the psychological condition caused by spending too much time in the Faroe Islands.

## Graves and Roses

The soldiers who died during the British occupation were buried in the cemeteries around the islands. In many of these cemeteries, memorial statues are raised to remember the soldiers who died during the war. Like in British military tradition, there were planted English roses in front of the gravestones so that when the sun was rising and setting throughout the day, the shadow of the roses would at some point be lying on the graves of the fallen soldiers.

## Merkið - Recognition of the Faroese Flag

Initially drawn in 1917 by Faroese students studying in Copenhagen, Denmark, the Faroese flag Merkið was first known as the student flag. Even though the students insisted this be the official Faroese flag and that many Faroese people took it to them and used it on their boats and their flagpoles, the Danish authorities never recognised the flag.

Since the Faroe Islands and Denmark were occupied by the two enemies, Great Brittain and Germany, it became a dangerous affair for the Faroese fishing vessels to sail under the Danish flag. Because of this inconvenience for the Faroese fishing vessels and because of safety measures, Merkið gained its formal recognition on the 25th of March 1940 by the British military, making it possible to differentiate between Danish and Faroese fishing vessels and ships.

**English Food and Candy**

Even though many years have passed since World War II ended, the influence of the British troops can still be seen today. The roads the British built are still very much in use but have, of course, been updated, and the airport is still located at the same site that the British chose during the occupation.

Those who were children during the war have told many stories about the English soldiers and that they had candy and chocolate, which they sometimes gave to the children. Back then, chocolate and even fruit were rare on the islands, and therefore the children were all very excited when they got these goods from the soldiers.

Even though most of the imported goods that come to the Faroe Islands come via Denmark, a considerable proportion of biscuits, tea, candy, and chocolate are still being imported from the United Kingdom, which is why there are many English brands otherwise unknown to the rest of Europe that can be found in every Faroese supermarket.

# The Death Penalty

## Is that still legal?

Historically, death penalties have been a part of the Faroese jurisdictional system and go back to Viking times. Though such penalties are believed to have been common, which the Færeyinga saga, the Viking traditions in general and some Faroese placenames indicate, nothing is recorded before the late 1500s.

In the 1600s, however, many recordings revealed that the penalties they used at that time were severe. People were often sentenced to long imprisonments, sometimes in holding cells with total darkness. The prisons have been located in several different places throughout Tórshavn, in Skansin (the old fort), Myrkastova (a basement in Tinganes) and other areas in Tinganes that today serve as parliament buildings. The sentences are believed to have been harsh, but people were usually let go when they reached their breaking point. Many men have been sentenced for work, sometimes for a specific period, other times for life. But, like in most other countries, people were sometimes also sentenced to death, and the harshest punishments recorded are death by hanging, drowning and beheading.

The first recorded death sentence was for a man from the island of Svínoy who was found guilty of incest. Though he is mentioned in "Jarðarbókin" from 1584, 1588 and 1590, nothing is known about his case. The assumption is, however, that he was executed in the local "Thing" in the northern islands. The oldest documented case was in 1615, when a man was sentenced for impregnating his wife's sister. They were both sentenced to death, and even though the means of their demise weren't mentioned, the man was expected to be beheaded, and the woman drowned.

Stealing was a severe crime, and the sentence for stealing sheep was death by hanging, and many such corrections have been for repetitive theft. According to the law, witchcraft was forbidden and sentenced to death by burning, but even though the law was n action and some were accused of witchcraft, no one was ever found guilty.

The last time someone was sentenced to death was in 1706 when two half-siblings from Streymoy conceived a child. They were both beheaded in Tórshavn.

Many of the sentences have been for incest, but the legal definition for incest, according to the law, was the relation in seven generations. This law was hard to uphold because the population at that time was low, which made it hard to follow this rule and still expand the population.

Often, when young women were sentenced to their death, the Faroese officials tried to postpone their judgement which they did by appealing to the Danish king. The far distance between the Faroes and Denmark meant that it took a long time to get a proper sentence in place, and when the king finally received the message and had decided on their fate, many had already fled the islands with foreign merchant ships.

Though the death penalty was the harshest sentence, many torture methods were used. It was common to see people flagged in public, where they would be stripped bare and whipped up to 39 times. Afterwards, the one whipped had to pull a chain with two large, heavy stones from the town centre and all the way to the outfields. This was to ensure that he or she would remember his or her misdeeds and so that they wouldn't commit the same crime they had done before.

Other scare tactics were also used. When someone was decapitated, the heads and sometimes other limbs were often attached to a pole outside the old fort to scare others into committing the same crime.

The executioner was paid handsomely. He was paid regularly and had a stable salary, and in addition, he would get paid extra whenever he had to execute a sentence, mild or harsh.

But society back then was small. Unlike in other countries, where the executioners could disguise their identity by wearing a mask, the executioner couldn't keep his identity a secret in the small town of Tórshavn. Therefore, it was difficult to get anyone to apply for the job, and sometimes when someone was sentenced to death, there wasn't anyone the execute the sentence. Therefore, he was sentenced to work as an executioner.

## The Sheep Letter

It is a widespread belief in the Faroe Islands that Seyðabrævið, the Sheep Letter, contains the death penalty for stealing sheep and that this law technically was in action until 2004, when the Sheep Letter was finally revoked. This is not true.

Seyðabrævið is dated the 28th of June 1298 and is the oldest document written on the Faroe Islands. Unlike the Færeyinga saga, which was written in Iceland only a few years prior, Seyðabrævið is written in Kirkjubø by the famous bishop Erlendur, who is known by some of the old legends. Erlendur was bishop in Kirkjubø and had the Kirkjubømúrurin built, which caused great outrage between the northern and the southern part of the Faroes. He demanded high taxes from the people, which started a civil war. According to the legend, he was killed during the war, but historical documents suggest that he fled to Norway around that time.

Seyðabrævið is a legal document from the early middle ages, and it exists in two original versions. One is kept in the National Archive in the Faroes, while the other is kept in a museum in Lund, Sweden, bound in a book with other historical Swedish documents from that time.

Contrary to popular belief, the letter contains no clause that authorises a death sentence. The idea hereof, however, might stem from mixing up the old practices of sentencing sheep theft and the letter regulating different sheep matters.

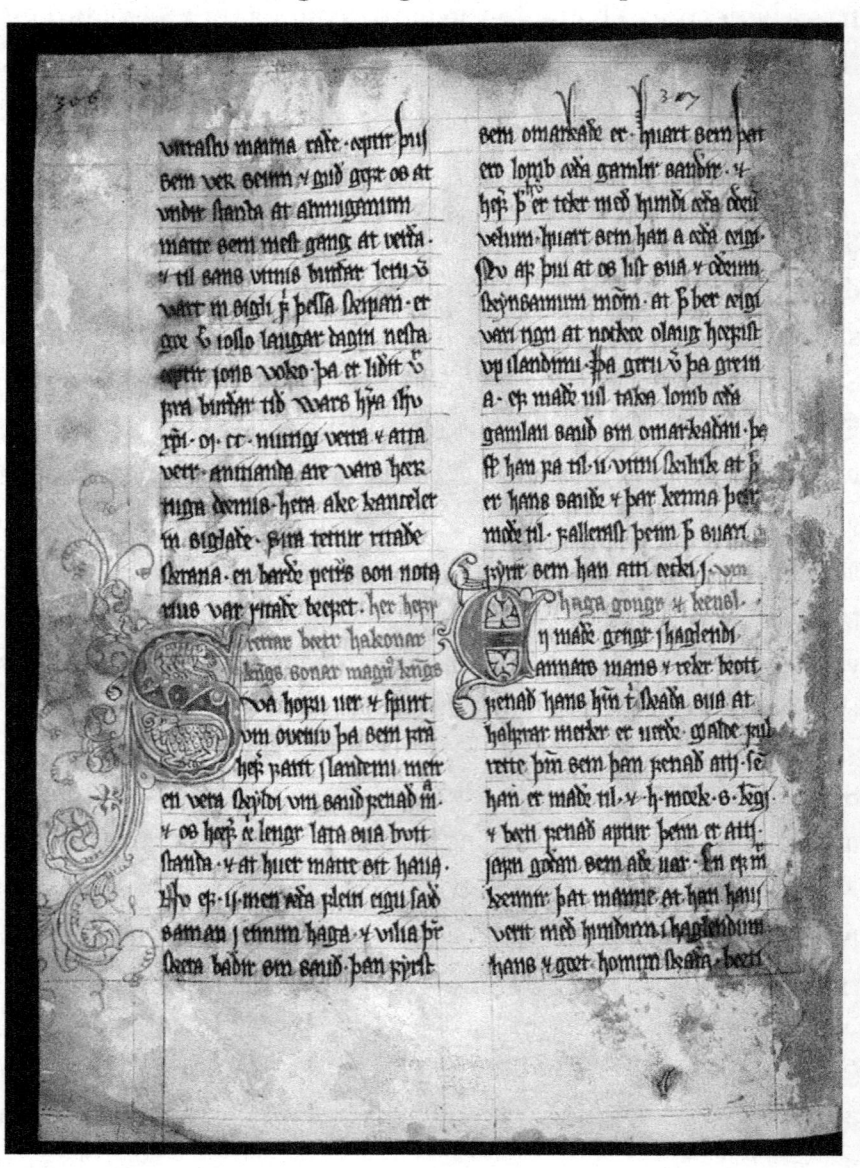

*The Sheep Letter*

## The Military Act from 1937

The old Danish Military Act from 1937 concerned all parts of the Kingdom, including the Faroe Islands and Greenland. When Denmark got a new law in 1973, the law did not concern the Faroe Islands, and therefore the 1937 law was still in action. § 37 in the Military Act from 1937 says as follows:

> *No life sentence may be carried out before the King[1] has decided not to exercise his right of pardon. The court that has handed down the final sentence must issue a statement on whether there is reason to recommend the convicted person for clemency. The execution will be postponed if the convicted person becomes insane.*

That meant that the death penalty could, in theory, still be upheld during times of war, though this was by extension to the Danish king, which in practice is the Folketing (Government).

In the 1990s, discussions started on whether the Faroe Islands should be included in the new Danish Military Act from 1973, which abolished Denmark's death penalty during war. This was part of a so-called "Ríkislógartilmæli", a recommendation concerning the Kingdom of Realm. But in 1992, the Faroese

---

[1] The King, in Danish law, is interpreted as the Danish Government.

Government declared it unsuiting to implement a Danish law in the Faroe Islands.

The recommendation of abolishing the 1937 Military Act was put forth again in the early 2000s. On the 22nd of November 2001, it was adopted without any opposing vote, though it was without adopting the 1973 law. An official statement was sent to the Danish Ministry of Justice on the 4th of December 2001, and the death penalty was now entirely abolished. Or so they thought.

The Faroe Islands even took a step further and discussed declaring the *European Convention on Human Rights*, which according to Protocol No. 13, abolishes the death penalty in all circumstances. This was adopted on the 21st of February 2002. But, as it turned out, the letter sent to the Ministry of Justice was nowhere to be found, and in March 2003, the 1937 Military Act was still not cancelled, and therefore the death penalty was still part of the Faroese regulation. It was then agreed to send another letter to Denmark to resolve these matters, and the law was then formally abolished.

# Religion and Superstition

## The Beliefs of the Faroe Islanders

The Faroe Islands is a very religious country. Approximately 80% are part of the State Church, while another 10% are affiliated with the free churches, whilst the other 10% either subscribe to other religions or are atheists. Even though people are leaving the church, now more than ever, the population growth sustains these numbers. This means that the number of churchgoers is steadily increasing, although the number of people leaving the church is also increasing.

The Faroe Islands are way more religious than the other Nordic countries. Studies within religion have shown that if one should find another country compared with the Faroe Islands, one has to look to the United States of America, which is the country in the Western world most comparable to the Faroes when it comes to religiosity.

Faroese people tend to be quite conservative, which highly correlates with religious belief. However, in recent years, the

*The Church of Saksun*

younger generations, with the influence of neighbouring countries, globalisation and trends accessible on the internet, the Faroe Islands have become more liberal, which can be seen in the legislation in 2016 that legalised same-sex marriages and in 2019 made adoptions legal for same-sex couples.

The current debate is focusing much on women's rights and the question of abortion, and like with the questions of same-sex marriages and the right to adopt for same-sex couples, the debates and discussions have been ongoing, with strong opinions and organisations advocating either side.

It is often stated that the Faroe Islands is a Christian nation, and even though the Faroes has no legislation saying that it is, some legislation, like, for instance, the legislation regarding the public school, states that schools must give students a moral Christian upbringing.

## Free Churches

The second largest Christian affiliation is the Brethren movement. In the late 1800s, it came to the Faroes from the Plymouth Baptist Church, which originates in southern England. Compared to the church, it was received as a miniature Christian revolution which broke from many of the church's traditions. Now it was possible to use other instruments during sermons, and Christian meetings were often held out in nature with people being baptised in lakes, rivers and even the sea.

But, the Brethren's also introduced a new perception of sin because whilst Faroese superstition and tradition had always co-existed with the Christian faith, some practices were now seen as sinful. Brethren were not allowed to participate in the Faroese chain dance, and trick and treating during easter was also considered a sin.

Biblical texts and psalms were translated into Faroese. Here, the Brethren movement played a significant role in developing written Faroese and using the Faroese language in general. The translations were extensive, and with the primary goal of making the Christian message accessible to regular people, the translations were also much easier to read. Here missionary Victor Danielsen (b. 1894 - d. 1961) translated 800 Psalms, 18 books and the Bible.

Today, there are many different free evangelic churches, many of which have strong ties to Christian movements in the United States of America. At the same time, other religious institutions like the Morman Church and Scientology have not been introduced yet. Even though Jews and Muslims live on the Faroes, there are no Jewish synagogues or Muslim mosques.

## The Folk-belief

In the olden days, people used to believe in ferries, pixies, hidden people (a form of elves), dwarfs, trolls, giants, mermaids, selkies, kelpies, nightmares and dwarfs. Today, these beliefs can be considered gone, but as late as the early 1900s, belief in different kinds of ghosts and people having special abilities was common. Some still hold these beliefs as accurate, but it can no longer be said that they are part of any popular belief.

Often, it is said that the trolls disappeared with the electricity. That is partly true because when the houses were modernised with modern kitchens, the social gatherings in the evenings that used to be an integral part of everyday life disappeared. At these social gatherings, people sang songs and told stories - many of whom were stories about the supernatural.

Back then, people used to believe in all sorts of mythical beings, which to them, were as accurate as their belief in God. But, even though superstitious beliefs and Christianity often are seen as counter opposites, the two sets of beliefs co-existed.

In the Faroese interpretation of Christianity, nothing prohibited these two world views from existing simultaneously; instead, they were entwined with the belief in God, who was used to protect the dangerous creatures living amongst them. This is evident in some of the magic spells that have survived through time, where the name of God has been part of protection spells, and so forth.

Even though the superstitious beliefs have vanished, they continue to influence the Faroese art scene; in music, fine arts and books.

# The Language and the Nobel Prize

## Recognition, both so and so

Although the Faroese language is closely related to the Old Norse language and is ancient, the Faroese written language is only a little over 150 years old. Faroese people could read and write in the Viking Age, as some of the country's oldest documents suggest. Still, the written language fell into the background over time and disappeared completely in the early Middle Ages.

Under the Danish king, it was mandated that Danish should be used in the church and schools. The Faroe Islands were then considered a Danish county because, at that time, the Faroe Islands were considered part of Denmark, similar to places like Bornholm and Southern Jutland.

Danish was considered finer than Faroese, and it was even claimed that God could not understand Faroese. Therefore, parts of the Faroese upper class insisted on speaking Danish instead of Faroese for several generations. But even though Faroese could not be accommodated in either the school or the church, the language has survived among the ordinary people, even if, by all the world's standards, it must be considered an endangered language, which a very limited population has only used. However, the language has always been in active use, which may have been the reason for the language's survival.

## The Recognition of the Written Language

In 1781 - 1782, the priest Jens Christian Svabo travelled in the Faroe Islands. He made an extensive collection of Faroese words and texts on his journey. But since there was no written language, he had to create his own language himself - this effort became the first bid for a reconstructed written language. Still, even though he made this effort, he was convinced that Danish had influenced the Faroese so much that the language would not survive over time. But Svabo's great effort meant that others were inspired to make similar collections.

In the 1820s, the first books were published in Faroese. These were ballads, biblical texts and the Færeyinga saga, translated by the priest Jóhan Hendrik Schrøter, also published in a language that was another attempt at a Faroese written language. However, some years passed before the Faroese language was reborn, and in 1846 the priest Venceslaus

*Picture of V. U. Hammershaimb*

Ulricus Hammershaimb introduced a common written language, which he had constructed with the great help of linguistic scholars from Denmark and Iceland. Instead of using a phonetic form, this language was based on the oldest forms of the language, with inspiration from Icelandic words and German grammar. With some adaptations, this became the language we know today as the written Faroese language.

But the language was much debated, and the recognition of the language still took many years until it was finally recognised among the Faroese. One of the language's critics was Dr Jakob Jakobsen, who had also done much collecting work. He believed that the language was too complicated to use and that a phonetic writing system would be more accessible for ordinary people to learn and use. He presented his proposal for a Faroese written language, but this caused great anger among those who were supporters of Hammershaimb's spelling and ended up not being adopted. However, books were also published in Jakobsen Faroese at this time.

It was only in 1938 that Faroese became part of the curriculum in primary schools, and in 1939 Faroese was accepted in the churches.

**William Heinesen and the Nobel Prize**

William Heinesen (b. 15th of January 1900 - d. 12th of March 1991) was a Faroese author, composer and artist.

He was born and raised in the Faroe Islands, where he lived most of his life except for some years when he was young. He wrote in Danish as this was the language he had been taught at home and in school. Therefore, the books he published were originally all written in Danish.

In his time, he was considered one of the most influential writers in Danish, and for that, he was considered to be nominated for the Nobel Prize in Literature in 1977.

*Picture of William Heinesen*

In addition to his literary work, Heinesen is considered among the best artists from the Faroes, and his works mainly revolve around Faroese myth and folklore. He was a pronounced art critic in the artistic subculture, and many have drawn inspiration from his creative paintings and works.

THE OBSCURE AND FUN FACTS OF THE FAROE ISLANDS

# Cartology and the Faroes

## Floating Islands and Fictive Countries

It is relatively common to see modern maps that do not include the Faroe Islands. This is the case both in physical and electronic maps. The Faroe Islands have had significant issues with shipping because the Faroe Islands are not included on several websites that supposedly ship worldwide. When it comes to large cooperations such as Google, it has also been a challenge to get the Faroe Islands included in Google Maps, which, however, was made possible by a campaign by the Faroese tourist bureau, Visit Faroe Islands, after the campaign known as "Sheep View".

But the Faroe Islands are very tiny, and the political landscape of not being a sovereign state while still having self-rule doesn't help in the general international recognition. Therefore, it is understandable by most that people out in the world haven't heard of the islands, and consequently, it is also understandable that the peninsula gets left out on some of the world's maps out there. But, even though this is something that keeps recurring, the Faroe Islands do appear on some of the maps stemming from the middle ages.

## Frislandia

In the so-called Zeno map, a map of the North Atlantic Ocean from around 1400 made by the Italian brothers Nicolò and Antonio Zeno, there is an island to the West of the Faroe Islands. The island is called Frislandia and is an island that has either never existed or has been mistaken for some of the existing islands in the North Atlantic.

The brothers claimed to have been on a voyage in the 1390s and had supposedly spent some time on the island of Frisland. Archival documents do, however, suggest that the Zeno brothers were in Venice, Italy, when their journey up north was said to have taken place, and today the Zeno map is being considered a hoax by most scholars.

When Nicolò Zeno published the map, it was widely accepted as accurate. Because of cartologists' method when producing maps of the world then, the island of Frisland would appear on virtually all maps from the 1560s to 1660s.

Those who believe the Zeno brothers' claimed journey have been debating whether or not the island of Frisland has been a forgery or if the brothers have mistaken this island for

Iceland, Southern Greenland, Northern Scotland, the Shetland Islands or the Faroe Islands. At different times these countries have all claimed to be the one country depicted as Frisland.

A case can be made that the Zeno brothers did mistake Frisland for the southern part of the Faroes because of the people who lived there around the same time as the brothers. During the 1400s, on the southernmost part of the Faroe Islands, legend tells of a Frisian colony (from Germany or the Netherlands) living in and around the area today known as Akraberg. These people lived separately from the rest of the Faroe Islanders and had distinct cultures. The legends surrounding these Frisians are all presumed to be from around 1300 and 1350, though some believe they have lived there since 700 or 800. If, say, the Zeno brothers visited this part of the Faroe Islands in the 1390s, it is plausible that they have met some of those who had survived the Black Plague that ravaged the Faroes in the mid-1300s, and which is said to have extinguished most of the Frisians. If that were the case, that would explain the name Frislandia.

However, the Frisian colonists are believed to have moved north because of political disputes, not only to the Faroes but also to the British Isles, Scandinavia and Iceland.

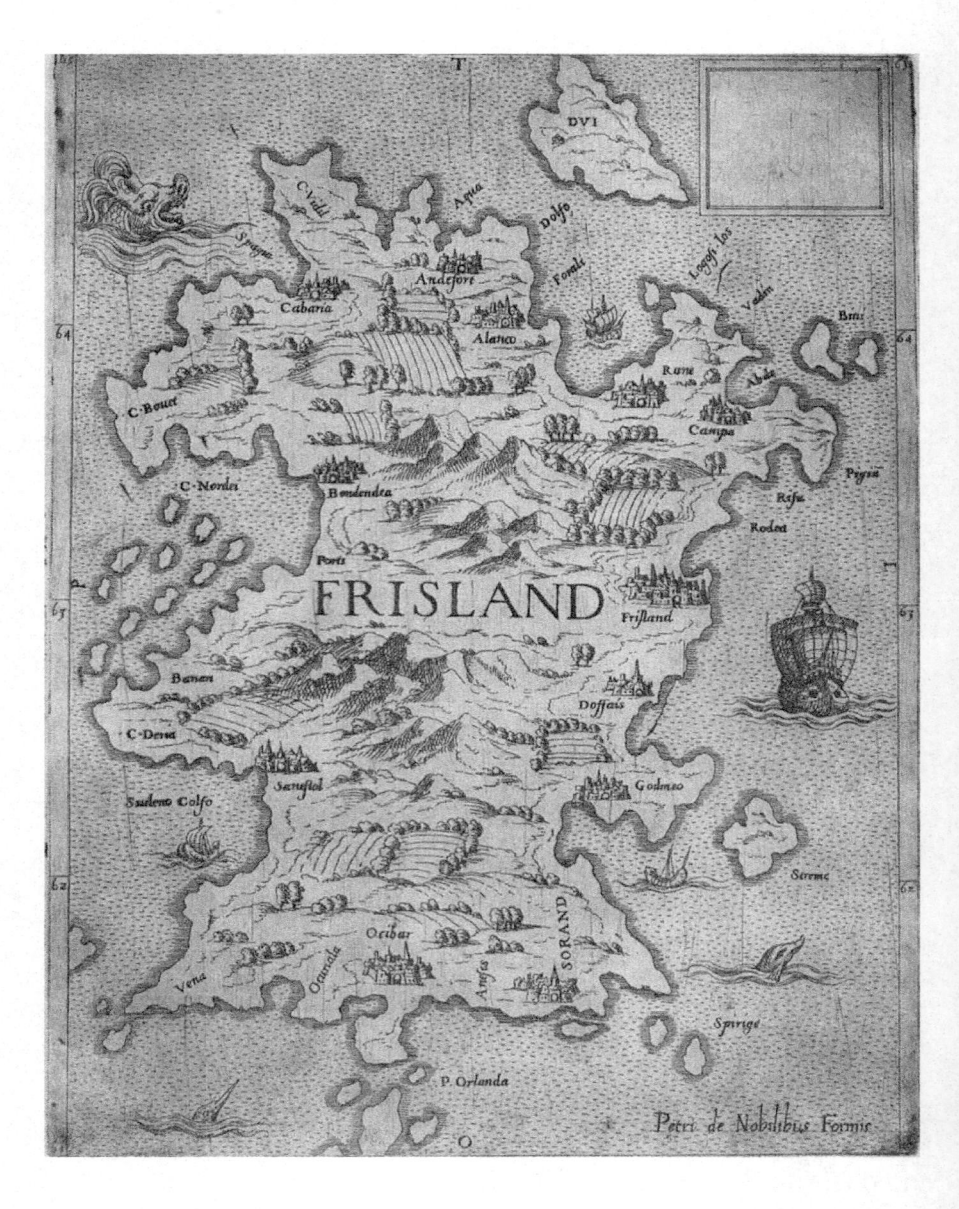

*Map of Frisland*

## Floating Islands

There are many legends surrounding the islands of the Faroe Islands. Many of them are said to have been floating islands which have been floating about in the North Atlantic Ocean. In the days of the priest Lucas Debes (b. 1623 - d. 1675), floating islands were still believed to exist, which is evident in one of the passages in his book Færoæ & Færoæ Reserata from 1673 where he writes of an account where a ship had passed an island in the south-east of the Faroes. In those waters, there was no known island, and the crew on the ship believed that island to be a floating island, and reading Debes' reflections, even though he is sceptical of floating islands, he was entertaining the idea. In his reflections on this stated account, he reflects on icebergs drifting from the North Pole and on another island, Enckhuyser Eyland, discovered near Iceland by the Dutch, which has since disappeared.

THE OBSCURE AND FUN FACTS OF THE FAROE ISLANDS

# Animal Life

## Extinction and Nearly Extinction

When the Vikings first arrived in the Faroes, the islands had a rich birdlife, and sheep and horses were already living on the islands. No one knows how these animals first came to the islands. Still, the original Faroese sheep breed is believed to be closely related to the breed that lives on Soay in the Outer Hebrides in Scotland, and the horse breed is closely related to the Shetland Pony. Therefore, it is believed that the first domestic animals arrived in the Faroes by the Irish monks, though they can have been brought by the people who were on the islands a few hundred years earlier, which nothing is known about.

In this chapter, I will introduce some of the most interesting stories and explanations of animals from the islands. But I have decided not to include other animals, such as the Faroese duck and the Faroese chicken, because close to nothing is written about these animals, and they still need to be investigated to determine whether they are a Faroese breed, as many do believe.

## The Faroese Horse

The Faroese horse is a small type of horse whose origin is unknown. Some believe they arrived with the Viking settlements, while others believe they were brought to the Faroes with the Irish monks that settled on the islands some hundred years before. In the 1950s, a Scottish veterinarian, James Speed, researched the breed and concluded that the breed originated from the breed that was common in North Scotland until the year 850, when a law was set in action which prohibited people from eating horse meat. Because of this law, the north Scottish breed was exported to Iceland and the Faroe Islands. This explanation seems plausible, but it is the only research that has been done on the topic.

In 1987 the Danish advisor on horse breeding Henning Rasmussen wrote the following description:

> *"The Faroese horse is a small, harmonious and attractive horse (pony) with relative depth and width. It has a well-shaped dry and expressive head. Mostly a little short, but well-set neck. The shoulder and mane area form a good saddle bearing. It has a strong topline, muscular and well-shaped - regularly a little short - croup and good thigh muscles. The limbs are relatively leaden and dry and predominantly fit, but a French pretence occurs. Throughout its knee and hocks are well marked and the breed has extremely good hooves with good horn quality.*

*The movement is predominantly energetic and light. The Faroese horse is known as a very enduring horse that can carry a relatively large weight and is also very safe on its feet."*

In the 1800s, around 800 individual horses lived on the Faroe Islands, mainly used for everyday work. From 1850 to 1900, the horses had a high selling value and were sold to Great Britain to work in the coal mine industry. Their small size and incredible strength made them perfect for the coal industry as they were used to shove the coal wagons in the mines. When most of the horses were sold off, there was simultaneously an increasing interest among the Faroe Islanders in importing new horse breeds, which people found much more desirable than the original horse. This made selling the Faroese horses even worse for the species that used to populate the islands. Eventually, nearly no pure breeds were left, and the horses were ultimately believed to be extinct. From this, some say that the saying "to make a horse trade" (i.e., a temporary advantage which in the long term proves to be a disadvantage) originates and refers to the unsustainable trades which almost ended up making the breed entirely extinct. This saying is, however, well-known in other languages, and there is no reason to believe that this saying has anything to do with the selling off of Faroese horses, even though it fits.

In the 1960s, people started to get interested in the horse again, but believing they were extinct, people tried looking to

*Faroese horse, picture presumably taken in Tórshavn*

see if they could find any horses left that no one knew about. When they started looking, they found only five individuals, of whom only one was male, and three of the female horses were all descendants from the fourth female horse, an old mare from the island of Vágar. The people who had led the investigation now saw that if the horses were to survive, they had to act instantly.

Today the Faroese Pony is still endangered and has only 87 individual horses (numbers from 2023). The local association, *Føroyska Rossið*, the Faroese Horse, and *Felagið Føroysk Ross*, The Faroese Horse Association, is working to sustain the population. Still, it has great worries about its endangerments and specific traits that only a few of the horses have, which derive from a particular genome which is hard to breed.

Unfortunately, the association has pressured politicians who have not called for action.

## The Faroese Cow

It is believed that the Faroese cow was brought to the islands with the first settlers. No one knows whether it was the Irish monks or the Norwegian Vikings, but it is believed to be of Norwegian descent, which indicates that it most likely was brought by the Vikings. But the Faroese cow was, however, its own breed, and like the horse, it was smaller than cattle from the neighbouring countries.

Faroese politician and poet Rasmus Effersøe was the first to describe the breed. He described it as small and short-legged, with short horns and mainly black.

When milk machines were introduced in the Faroe Islands, modern machines were not suited for small cows. Therefore, farmers started cross-breeding the cattle by importing from Denmark, Iceland, Norway and the United Kingdom. In 1987, some specimens that hadn't been crossbred were still left, but Hestur was the only island with bulls. Instead of preserving the original species, the cattle were introduced to specimens from Norway, and after that, none of the original cattle was ever born again.

Farmers were happy because the cross-breeding was so effective that it doubled the cow's milk.

*Young woman milking a cow*

In 2003 all cattle on the islands were inspected in search of the original species. From around 1.000 cows, there were eight specimens which seemed to closely resemble the original breed though it was evident that these had been crossed with other breeds. In hopes of conserving the remaining original genes, genome samples were collected and preserved for further investigation. With the genome, scientists hope to be able to reintroduce cattle more closely related to the original Faroese cow.

With the 2003 investigation, it was finally evident that the Faroese cow had, in fact, gone extinct.

## The Sheep of Dímun

The sheep known as the Dímunarseyður - the Sheep of Dímun - was the original breed of sheep that roamed the islands before the Norse Viking settlers arrived in the Faroes between the late 6th and late 8th century.

The sheep was a primitive short-tailed breed closely related to the sheep that live on the island of Soay in St. Kilda in the Outer Hebrides of Scotland. The sheep had short wool, which was not suited for knitting. Therefore, the islanders only learned knitting after introducing the breed of sheep that live on the islands today, presented in the 1600s.

The sheep survived on the island of Dímun while being extinct throughout the rest of the islands, and therefore, it was named after the island. Being isolated for so long, the sheep had become wild and hostile towards people, and when people from Hvalba and Sanvdík in Suðuroy bought the island in 1850, the remaining sheep of the island were shot. This was because the sheep were hard to capture, and men felt frightened of being rammed by the sheep and off the island's steep cliffs.

From some local legends in Sandoy, which have been written down in the 1970s, it is said that the sheep there sometimes have been hard to handle and have shown to be quite aggressive. It has therefore been believed that these sheep had interbred with the original breed of the island and that the sheep of Sandoy shared some of the genes of the Dímunarseyður.

Whether or not this is true, no one knows. The sheep breed that lives on the islands today all share some of the genes of the old breed. But there are some indications that the sheep of Sandoy might be more inbred with the original species, which is indicated by the old sheepfolds there. Unlike in other places throughout the islands, these sheepfolds have been partly dug into the ground, making a hole to trap the sheep in when the sheep are driven into the fold. That way, it is more difficult for the sheep to escape than in any regular sheepfold.

**The White Raven**

The White-Pied Raven, Hvítravnur, was a white-pigmented raven that used to live in the Faroe Islands. It was the same race as the black ravens that live on the islands today, but due to a gene malfunction, the pigments had changed for some of them, which turned their colour white and brown. The pied raven was only found on the Faroe Islands, even though the breed was closely related to the North Atlantic species.

*The White Pied Raven*

Like the Faroese horse, people abroad became eager to get their hands on the pied raven. Prices for stuffed examples were high, so they were highly demanded.

Before and during the spiked interest for this bird, a system ordered anyone to deliver the beaks of ravens and eagles once a year towards payment. This was to control the population of these birds that were harmful to young sheep, especially in the spring and had a considerable impact on the food resources that the islanders depended so much upon. This system eventually ended the sea eagle, which was nesting in a few hard-to-reach places in the country, but the pied raven was so common that its population was not considered threatened. The interest in Europe, however, caused the last white raven to be shot in 1902, some examples were seen after that; the last one was seen in 1948.

**Whales and Whaling**

One cannot talk about animals in the Faroe Islands without also mentioning whales and the controversial whale-hunting tradition of the islands, known as the grind.

The Faroese have hunted whales since before recorded Faroese history, though it is mentioned in the Sheep Letter from 1298. It is most likely a tradition that goes as far back as Viking times, but statistics have been made from each whale hunt since 1584, the oldest unbroken statistic in the world.

The whales being hunted are primarily pilot whales, and sometimes also North Atlantic dolphins, and the hunt itself is only the pots of whales that swim between the islands -

whalers do not go to sea to search for whales. When fishing vessels sail by a pot of whales, they are not driven towards the shores.

*Four whalers participating in a whalehunt*

The whale hunt is a bloody affair, as one might imagine when such large animals are slaughtered in the free and sea. Whales are large and contain a lot of blood; therefore, the sea gets red during the slaughter.

But, though it might be dramatic, the slaughter is perceived as a natural part of life, and it is common to see children participate in the slaughter; this is not a harmful or traumatising experience for the children.

In recent years the Faroe Islands have experienced increased pressure from animal welfare activists, who have tried to put a full stop to the whale hunt, but without succeeding. Some activist organisations have been known to use rather extreme methods to stop the grind by making one-sided documentaries which, to the Faroese, have been perceived as dishonest and disrupting the hunt using speed boats. In fact, during one of these attempts, crew members from the organisation Sea Shepherd were fined for animal cruelty because the propeller of their speed boats had sliced up several whales when they were sailing back and forth to disrupt the whale hunt.

But, the focus on animal welfare has also impacted methods used for slaughter; some tools have been banned, and some new tools have been invented. In only a few years, a unique spear was developed, which paralyses the whale instantly by piercing it into the whale's blow hole, making the killing more humane. Also, since 2013 anyone who participates in a whale slaughter has to have a licence which one can get by attending a whale slaughtering course.

The whaling tradition is a solidary system where anyone who participates gets their share of the catch. Sometimes everyone from a village also gets their share of the catch.

Due to heavy metal pollution, fewer and fewer young people eat whale meat. Whale meat is not recommended as food for young people of fertile age by the authorities, as mercury pollution settles in the body and can be inherited by newborns. At the same time, some young people distance themselves from whaling, as many are against meat production by being vegan or vegetarian.

# THE OBSCURE AND FUN FACTS OF THE FAROE ISLANDS

## Challenging Delicacies

Potatoes, something rotten and potatoes again

The Faroese kitchen, to a foreigner, must be rather extreme. It's hard to talk about culture without mentioning the food associated with it. Due to the lack of agriculture and the wet climate, the Faroes have developed some peculiar food traditions using conservation methods that are quite different from the rest of Europe.

In the olden days, before refrigerators, there were only a few ways to preserve food that had been caught. Meat and fish were preserved using either salt or drying methods for fermentation, using the wind and the wet climate.

Fermented Faroese food has a strong smell to it, and a strong taste as well. Though it might be an acquired taste, most Faroese people perceive this kind of food as special delicacies, and to anyone who hasn't tried it, it is certainly an experience which you cannot try other places in the world.

The Faroese cold and wet climate with a stable temperature throughout the year makes for optimal conditions for fermenting meat and fish. Traditionally, this kind of food is served with beer and aquavit (a Scandinavian kind of spirit), but is excellent with sea infused single malt whiskey, such as Talisker Whiskey or other kinds of whiskeys from the Scottish coast line or islands.

**Roots and potatoes**

In the olden days, when the Faroe Islands was still a Danish county, the King demanded that all farmers pay their taxes using corn stock. But, as the weather on the Faroe Islands was cold, wet and harsh, the farmers struggled to get their crops growing. It was possible to grow corn, but it was very ineffective, and the farmers struggled to get enough stock to pay what they owed to the King.

Farmers could use their land much more efficiently with the potato's introduction. Just as it did in Ireland, it changed what the farmers could deliver in taxes to the King because while the corn was tough to manage, the potatoes were much easier to maintain and seemed to flourish in the Faroese climate.

The first time the potato was documented was in 1686, and how it is mentioned suggests that it was common at that point. It is believed that roots were introduced simultaneously. When the potato was first introduced, it got prevalent and soon, potato fields were a common sight around the islands. In some places, one can see how the people have cleared the mountainsides for potato harvesting and removed entire mountains for rocks and stones.

If there is anything that defines any traditional Faroese dish, it is the potato. No matter what recipe, it will most likely, contain potatoes.

**Salted food**

One of the food-preserving methods is using salt. It is common to have a large barrel in the drying sheds with whale meat and blubber; some also have such barrels with fish.

In the olden days, making salted fish and exporting it primarily to Spain was common. Here, it is said that the Faroese brought the Bacalao tradition to Spain, though this idea has yet to be confirmed. If that is true, then the Spaniards must be said to have experimented with and evolved it because, in the Faroes, salted fish is typically served in the same way as it has always been with potatoes and sweet-sour sauce.

THE OBSCURE AND FUN FACTS OF THE FAROE ISLANDS

*Fermented fish hanging outside a drying shed*

## Fermented food

Ræst kjøt and ræstur fiskur are two Faroese delicacies distinct in taste and smell. Ræst kjøt is fermented sheep meat and ræstur fiskur is fermented fish. Even though it isn't as common as it used to be, whale meat, primarily the ribs, is sometimes also fermented.

Fermentation is a rotting process that preserves food by handing it up to dry. In other cultures, we know fermentation from preserving vegetables like kimchi and sauerkraut. In the Faroes, however, it has traditionally been fish or meat when something is fermented.

The meat is dried in a drying shed with barred walls where the wind can blow through, keeping the meat away from the rain while being dried over a long period by the salty breeze. When the food is ready, it has a strong smell and a solid aromatic taste, which many tourists have often found off-putting. However, the locals love it and associate it with the festive seasons.

THE OBSCURE AND FUN FACTS OF THE FAROE ISLANDS

## Faroese Currencies

LEGO money or a predecessor to Cryptocurrency?

The currency of the Faroe Islands is the Danish krone which closely follows the Euro. Even though Faroese paper money could make one believe that the money is Faroese, it has a distinct design and gets printed by the Faroese banks. However, this is not true since its currency is entirely Danish, and the coins used are Danish.

During World War II, the Danish money applicable on the islands was made distinct by being stamped with red ink saying: "*Kun gyldig paa Færøerne. Færø Amt, Juni 1940*," translated "*Only valid on the Faroe Islands. Faroe County, June 1940.*" By stamping the paper money, the Faroes could separate their currency from that of Denmark, which Germany occupied then. Like with paper money, coins were also drilled into separating the coins. The stamped paper money and drilled coins were the only valid currency on the islands and could not be used in Denmark and vice versa.

## Privately owned currencies

Like crypto valuta today, there used to be currencies alternative to the currency that was backed by the state. These were privately owned by companies who, in the years 1929 to 1933, when the Faroe Islands were in a deep financial crisis, tried to solve the problem of simply having too few coins fluctuating in the society which caused enormous problems for the companies when they had to pay their workers. To solve this problem, the companies started with a booking system where the workers had to register their working hours where a given amount of hours resulted in vouchers that could only be used in stores owned by the company they worked for.

At that time, the companies owned the fishing vessels, the fish factories and the drugstores, making the workers entirely dependent on them regarding their income and everyday spending.

The newly implemented booking system quickly resulted in the workers registering too many working hours compared to how much they had worked. The companies then tried another system where workers and employers would register the hours daily. When these numbers didn't add up it caused immense dissatisfaction and a lot of quarrels between employers and employees.

Clergyman Samuel Peter Petersen in Fuglafjørður then got the idea of making his own set of coins to pay his workers, which he had made in a factory in Bilbao, Spain, that specialised in making tokens for casinos. The authorities did not recognise the coins, which could only be used at his personal store. These coins solved the problems the booking system couldn't, and already a year later, in 1930, clergyman Jógvan Fredrik Kjølbro from Klaksvík had copied S. P. Petersen's idea for his own company J. F. Kjølbro.

Even though the Danish state did not recognise the coins, people grew confident in the actual value the coins represented since they could be used for goods in the stores. Seeing that the trust had been put in these currencies, people started trading the different coins, which increased the demand for the coins - so much so that official Danish krones often were traded because they had no higher value in practice.

The private currencies took a quick end when they, in 1933, were banned by Danish authorities who confiscated all the coins from both companies by gathering them together and throwing them into the sea.

# THE OBSCURE AND FUN FACTS OF THE FAROE ISLANDS

*Coins by Kjølbro*

*Coins by S. P. Petersen*

**Coins by J. F. Kjølbro, Klaksvík** (1930 - 1933).

- 10 øre
- 25 øre
- 50 øre
- 1 krone
- 2 krone
- 5 krone
- 10 krone

The coins had a round shape and varied in sizes.

**Coins by S. P. Petersens Eftf, Fuglafjørður** (1929 - 1933).

- 5 øre
- 10 øre
- 25 øre
- 1 krone
- 2 krone
- 5 krone

The coins were made of brass and varied in shape and size, with some containing extensive writing and some small. Some had the writing EPTF and some EFTF.

THE OBSCURE AND FUN FACTS OF THE FAROE ISLANDS

# Vehicles and Vessels

## Barrel Vehicles and Mountain-built Catamarans

Even though the Faroe Islands have nearly no trees, an old boat-building tradition goes far back to the Viking age. The boats that have been built have been made from driftwood, imported wood and wood that has washed ashore from shipwrecks.

It is said that the first Faroese ship, Royndin Fríða, was built in Vágur in the early 1800s. This ship was built from recycled wood from an English cargo vessel abandoned in the Faroes because of its poor shape. The Faroese national hero, Nólsoyar Páll, bought the wreckage at an auction, and with it, he built Royndin Fríða with help from four other men.

### The Traditional Faroese Boat

The traditional Faroese boat is derived from the Norn clinker boat. Still, through the ages, the Faroese boat has been adapted to Faroese needs which have been fisheries, whale hunting and transporting goods and livestock between the islands. Boatbuilding is a tradition passed down through the generations where the elder boat builders have taught the younger ones and have never been part of any formalised education.

Even though the Faroese boat is still being built for the traditional Faroese rowing sport, the demand for such boats is deficient. Modern fibreglass boats are better suited for harsh weather conditions and are geared with modern equipment. Building such boats takes hundreds of hours and is therefore of very high-end quality and expensive. This has caused a decline in new boats being built. Additionally, it must be said that only ten boat builders who know the old building tradition are left. With the lack of apprentices to carry on with this tradition, the Faroese boat must be considered to be highly threatened.

In a report from 2012, the Ministry of Culture estimated that the boat-building tradition might be lost in about 20 years if the younger generation doesn't take up this tradition. But, there might still be hope because recently, there have been a handful of young men who have started as apprentices for boat building and also, on the 14th of December 2021, the traditional Faroese boat became part of the UNESCO World Heritage List together with the conventional clinker boats from the other Nordic countries.

## Boatbuilding in a Mountain Village

KJ Hydraulik was founded in 1978 as a small mechanical workshop in Fuglafjørður focusing on hydraulic systems and has since expanded into the largest mechanical workshop on the Faroe Islands, specialising in hydraulics but in the salmon industry as well.

Today it has three central departments: the Administrative department, the Sales department and the Technical department, with the third mentioned having four subdivisions: the Mechanical shop, the Forklift division, the Entrepreneur division and the Automatic division.

In the late 80s, the workshop moved to the mountain village of Kambsdalur, a satellite village from Fuglafjørður. In this mountain village, some 135 meters above sea level, KJ Hydraulik has a boatbuilding shop that produces high-quality catamarans designed for salmon farming, which the firm exports to salmon farmers worldwide.

Seeing that this all happens in a mountain village when the boats are set afloat, they get transported by large trailers from Kambsdalur to the neighbouring town of Fuglafjørður. When this happens, the roads get closed, and sometimes they have had to remove light posts to make space for transporting the larger models through the town and to the dock.

*Catamaran being pulled by a trailer*

## The Danga

It is said that when Faroese fishermen first came to England to buy the wooden schooners, which made it possible for them to go far out to sea to their fisheries, they bought vessels, which they called Danga. Danga is a common Faroese word today, and the meaning of this word is something like "an old wooden, beaten-up ship."

The vessels they bought were all labelled with signs saying "Danger," and because the Faroese were so bad at English, they mistook these signs for being a type of vessel instead of a ship in poor shape.

This story has often been told as a joke, but in Dr Tórður Jóansson's doctorate thesis about English loanwords in Faroese, he argues that the story is true. Linguists and historians tend to agree with Dr Jóansson even though the account has many variations.

## The "Dream Car"

In the 1950s, a Norwegian man called Almar Nordhaug built a car that he named the Dream Car (Later, in Norway, the Aeroplane). With help from colleagues, Nordhaug had the car built in a barrel factory in Tórshavn, and when it was finished, its futuristic design was of much amusement for the locals when it was seen driving in the streets of Tórshavn and the Faroe Islands in general.

The car was based on the Vauxhall Cresta chassis, drivetrain and engine, and its design took great inspiration from the 1954 Ford concept car called the FX-Atmos. Its handmade body and roof, taken from an aeroplane, made it look like something from a 1950s sci-fi sitcom. It also had loudspeakers and a cassette player, which was something that had never

*The Dream Car driven by Nordhaug*

been seen before, adding to the car's innovative and futuristic feel.

Nordhaug drove around in his homemade vehicle for a while, but eventually, he moved back to Norway in 1957 and brought the car with him. There, he also drove the car for some years, but already in the early 60s, the car was set for sale and was in bad condition. It was bought at a used car dealership by Nils Petter Weiberg Aurdal, who restored the car and then sold it again to a furniture company in Oslo called Grefa, which used it as a display car.

What happened to the car in the end, nobody knows. There are contradicting rumours: some say that the vehicle was destroyed some years ago while others still believe it to be kept safe somewhere.

## Faroese Custom cars

One of the most famous custom carmakers is Sofus Hansen in Tórshavn. Throughout his life, he has rebuilt many different car models; his rebuilds are not regular customisations, but with his great eye for detail and high skills as a modifier, his rebuilds are pure design transformations.

In his home garage, he has his workshop, where his rebuilds have all been made. In the early years, he kept his work modest, mixing a Volkswagen Beetle with a Rolls Royce and rebuilding a Chevrolet Stingray into something resembling the 1989 Batmobile. But he has taken his building to a new level in recent years.

One of his most famous rebuilds has been a Porsche 928 S4 from 1991. For this build, he won a prize in Sweden for the best custom build car and was making the headlines there in the car magazines.

# THE OBSCURE AND FUN FACTS OF THE FAROE ISLANDS

# Cinematography and Movies

## And the Death of James Bond

In recent years the Faroe Islands have become an increasingly popular scenery for cinematics in the film industry. Even though it was rumoured to be scheduled as one of the filming locations for Peter Jackson's The Lord of the Rings trilogy, this rumour has never been confirmed even though it is easy to imagine with the beautiful scenery and unspoiled nature. But scenes from the Faroes have since been used for films such as *Submergence* (2017) starring Alicia Vikander and James McAvoy and series such as *Trom* (2022) starring Ulrik Thomsen and Faroese actor Olaf Johannesen. The islet of Tindhólmur has also been used in the series *His Dark Materials* (2019) and serves as the island where the witches live, and in the new Disney production of *Peter Pan & Wendy* (2023), scenes have also been used in some of the islands, cliffs and sea stacks. The most extensive film set that has ever been to the Faroe Islands is, without question, the *James Bond* movie, *No Time to Die*, which hit the cinema in 2021.

## No Time to Die

The movie *No Time to Die* (2021) is Daniel Craig's last movie as James Bond. This is evident at the movie's end when Bond dies from a large missile strike after realising that he was infected by nanobots which makes him unable to touch his daughter Mathilde or his beloved Madeliene, played by actress Léa Seydoux.

Like the other Bond films, No Time to Die has an extensive range of filming locations, one of them being on the Faroe Islands, which is the location that serves as the death place of 007.

In the movie, the villain's island is supposed to be a Japanese island, but its filming location is actually in a place called Kallur which is on the northernmost part of the island of Kallsoy.

On the place where Agent 007 died now resides a tombstone which says the following:

IN MEMORY OF

JAMES BOND 1962 - 2021

THE PROPER FUNCTION OF MAN IS TO LIVE, NOT EXIST.

*James Bond's mock tombstone, Kalsoy*

The mock tombstone was erected on the 21st of March 2022 by the farmer of Trøllanes, Jóhannus Kallsgarð, which owns the land where the scenes were shot and who is credited in the movie's end credits as "King of Kallsoy."

The quote on the tombstone is the words that M, played by actor Ralph Fiennies, reads at Bond's funeral in the end scene of the movie *No Time to Die* from 2021. The full quote is ascribed initially to the American author Jack London and goes as follows:

> "*The proper function of man is to live, not to exist. I shall not spend my days in trying to prolong them. I shall use my time.*"

Ian Flemming later used it to describe James Bond in the novel *You Only Live Twice* (1964), where the world at one point thinks that Bond has died. The quote is the end part of Jack London's original writing, which goes as follows:

> *"I would rather be ashes than dust! I would rather that my spark should burn out in a brilliant blaze than it should be stifled by dry-rot. I would rather be a superb meteor, every atom of me in magnificent glow, than a sleepy and permanent planet. The proper function of man is to live, not to exist. I shall not waste my days in trying to prolong them. I shall use my time."*

## Skyfall

Even though *No Time to Die* was the first time the James Bond franchise was in the Faroe Islands, there's reason to believe that the James Bond movies have had influence deriving from the Faroes.

In his lifetime Ian Flemming only wrote 14 novels and nine short stories about the James Bond character. Still, there have been 25 movie instalments on the big screen.

When Flemming died on the 12th of August 1964, some of his short stories, which are included in the nine mentioned stories, were published posthumously. After his death, other authors continued writing about Agent 007. Some of these post publications have been the novels behind movies such as *Licence to Kill* (1989), but even though many more James Bond titles are available, the movie *Skyfall* (2012) was not among these titles.

Instead, this movie takes great inspiration from another spy book - one from a book series about a character who has influenced James Bond before in the film *Moonraker* from 1979.

There are good reasons to believe that the storyline of *Skyfall* was highly inspired by John Buckham's 1939 novel *The Island of Sheep*. This idea was discussed in a 2019 Faroese article which analysed and compared the storyline in the book and the film. The article concludes that *Skyfall* is highly inspired by the book, which was supported by comparable coincidences in both stories, such as the story itself, place names, events and so on. The fact that John Buckham's books have inspired Ian Fleming further substantiates this point of view, in addition to the few original James Bond titles that have still not been used in the film series are limited. Therefore, this is also a good solution for a film company that intends to produce more James Bond films.

One of the lines from the article claims that: "[...] *he* (James Bond) *was here before we knew it.*"

# THE OBSCURE AND FUN FACTS OF THE FAROE ISLANDS

## Public Service and Bingo

### The Public Radio and Television Broadcasting Service

The National Public Service radio and television broadcaster, Kringvarp Føroya (KVF), is funded through demanded pay for anyone who has turned 18 years old. Even though the payment is demanded, it has been kept separate from the tax system securing funding without political interference.

Kringvarp Føroya was originally two different broadcasting services. The radio, Útvarp Føroya, was founded in 1957 and the television, Sjónvarp Føroya, in 1984. In 2005 these two public broadcasting services merged into one broadcasting station, which is part of the public service, comparable to BBC, but smaller.

As a public service, the broadcasting station is inclined to produce and broadcast a wide range of content, some of which have been to great amusement among the public.

## Gekkurin - a Cultural Treasure of playing Bingo

Every Friday at 8 pm, KVF has a bingo programme where people can play along in their homes via television. The programme is called Gekkur and is one of the national broadcaster's primary incomes. It has been running for more than 25 years (since February 1997) and is funded by sponsorship and by people who buy their bingo plates each week.

In this bingo programme, random numbers are shown on the television screen, and from home, people match these numbers with their bingo plates. In the first three games, players must get a row on one of the plates and then call to live television to select a letter. Behind these letters, the winners can choose between different gift vouchers. In the game's fourth round, players must get a full plate and then call the television programme. One of the lucky winners then gets to turn the Gekkur wheel of fortune, where they can win a relatively large sum of money.

The programme has shown to be so popular that it is a standard part of everyday conversation and small talk where the question often is asked: "Are you going to play Gekkur tonight?"

*The Gekkur wheel of fortune*

Due to its popularity, the programme sometimes has its own house band, which plays background music while the game of bingo is ongoing. The band is called Konfekt, and its band members are some of the most experienced and best-known musicians from the Faroe Islands who are known to have worked with artists such as Eivør and Teitur, etc.

The band has proven so popular that it attended the annual G! Festival in 2016 and the yearly Summarfestivalur in 2011, the two largest competing annual music festivals in the Faroe Islands.

## The Weather Forecast Broadcasting

Each day the weather forecast is broadcasted as part of the news program on radio and television. The weather forecast has been part of radio and television stations since the beginning. This stems from when the Faroe Islands only had Norwegian radio, and to this day, when people ask about the weather, they ask: *Hvat sigur norðmaðurin?* - What does the Norwegian guy say?

The old Faroese people used to be very interested in the weather conditions. When the radio first came to the Faroese and the weather broadcast reported lousy weather, the locals blamed the weathercast hosts.

## The Announcement of Deaths and Funerals

Each day at three o'clock, the names of every person diseased are read on the radio after the three o'clock news and can also be read on the website KVF.fo. The announcement covers the name, birth name, nickname, age, where they come from and where they lived. This includes residents living on the Faroes and people residing abroad. Here the funeral is also announced, and people can pay their respects by donating money to charity organisations or family members to cover the funeral costs, etc.

Sometimes, when a person of a particular public interest has been diseased, and the reporters need a news story, they make a profile depicting the person's life and their importance and contribution to society, etc.

## Christmas Greetings from Abroad

Every Christmas, the radio broadcasts Christmas greetings from Faroese people who live, study or work abroad. This old tradition is still followed, although the distances today are different from what they were when it initially came into effect.

Christmas greetings are trendy amongst the locals; for many, they are an integrated part of their annual Christmas traditions.

Some of these greetings are often cited where people make fun of the pronunciation of people who have lived abroad for a long time or children who haven't quite learned Faroese properly.

THE OBSCURE AND FUN FACTS OF THE FAROE ISLANDS

# World Records

## And Wild Achievements

Even though the Faroe Islands is a small country, and despite only having approximately 55.000 inhabitants, many wild and outstanding achievements have been made amongst the Faroese people, both in historical and modern times.

In this chapter, I will try to introduce many of these impressive achievements that people have made throughout the years, some of which are unbelievable. These are stories about Nobel Prize winners, the world's oldest siblings, a Faroese explorer who was one of the first Europeans ever to travel to Siberia, explorers of the sea, etc.

### The Nobel Prize in Medicine and Physiology

Niels Ryberg Finsen (b. 1860 - d. 1904) was a Faroese physician and scientist of Icelandic descent who, since 1903, is the only Faroese person ever to receive a Nobel Prize. However, William Heinesen, in the late 1970s, was nominated for one in literature, which he rejected.

*Painting of Niels R. Finsen*

Finsen was born and raised in Tórshavn, where he also started in school. But at an early age, he was sent to a boarding school in Herlufsholm in Denmark, where his older brother was also studying. He was estimated unsuited as a student because of his poor presentation and low grades. Therefore, he was sent to his father's old school in Iceland, where he continued his studies. In 1876, at the age of 21, he graduated in Iceland, but at his graduation, he was number 11 of 15 students.

In 1882 he moved to Copenhagen to study medicine. This time, however, he would show much more talent than he had shown earlier. After graduation, he became increasingly involved in teaching at the University of Copenhagen. Eventually, in 1898 he received his professorship but was at that point mainly focusing on his scientific research within the field of light therapy.

In 1903 he was awarded a Nobel Prize in Medicine and Physiology for his contribution to treating skin diseases using light radiation. He was the first person from the Faroes to be awarded the Nobel Prize and the first person in Scandinavia to get the prize.

Because of this, the Faroe Islands became the country in the world with the most Nobel Prize winners per capita, and to this day, it still is.

## Sigert, the Faroese Explorer

At the age of 20, in 1889, the young Faroese man from Kirkjubø, Sigert Patursson, left his home country to travel the world on a journey that eventually would have him spend many years in western Siberia.

He first came to Scotland, then Denmark and Sweden. In January 1990, he set for Siberia, an unexplored territory for most of Europe at that time, and life in Siberia was something that no one knew about. Since the region was unknown, there were no roads or railways, so he had to walk and use sledges on his journey.

When he arrived, he spent six years with the original inhabitants of Siberia. From his experience there, he wrote a twelve-bound book from 1900 to 1901, which sold well and sparked people's curiosity in Europe. After travelling in Siberia, he was invited to hold speeches and lectures across

Europe. Journalists took great interest in him everywhere he went and published many articles in the respective countries.

*Picture of Sigert Patursson*

He continued his travels holding lectures and visiting Norway, Finland, Russia and Sweden again. In Sweden and Norway, where he wrote his book, he also published many articles about his travels, which were very well received.

But exploring wasn't the only reason people took an interest in him. He was always very well dressed and had political ideas, which many thought radical. He dreamt of a joint world order where every nation would unite. He wrote and published articles on the topic and had ideas about psychology, pedagogics and esthetics, which he also wrote about.

Later, in 1907 he travelled to Mongolia, Korea, the Middle East, France, Poland, Egypt and many other countries, which was unusual for anyone citizen at that time. Still, for a Faroese person, it was unheard of.

He took his idea of a joint world seriously, and in his later writings, he would always sign them "Sigert Patursson the First of the World".

## Tróndur Paturson

Tróndur Patursson (b. 1944) is one of the most famous artists from the Faroe Islands. He has held art exhibitions worldwide and is a recognised name in the world of fine art paintings.

But, when Tróndur was young, he was also a seafarer and a prolific adventurer who had adventures on the world's seven seas.

Inspired by the legend of St. Brendan, who is said to be the first Irish monk to settle on the Faroe Islands, and who is said to not only have arrived by skin boat but travelling as far as the Americas, Tróndur decided to try and see whether it was possible to do such a voyage using such a boat.

In 1976 Tróndur and Tim Simerin decided to make the same voyage as St. Brendan, and with a boat built in the same fashion as leather boats from around the year 600, they sailed from the Faroe Islands to Iceland and then to Newfoundland. The boat was named Brandan after the Irish monk.

**Rowed Across the Atlantic Ocean**

In 2018 three Faroese men and a man from New Zealand set a new world record for rowing the furthest distance ever recorded. The men, Jákup Jacobsen, Jógvan Clementsen, Niclas Olsen and Isaac Giesen (NZ), left port in Portugal on the 10th of February, and 74 days later, they landed in Cuba on the 12th of May, after having rowed 8.000 kilometres in one go.

## Livar Nysted

Livar Nysted (b. 1970) is a Faroese painter and athlete. Even though he might be better known for his paintings, he has set several records in rowing. He started indoors rowing at 27 but eventually started rowing out on the fjords.

In 2013 he and two other men, Maxime Chaya from Libanon and Stuart Kershaw from England, crossed the Indian Ocean by rowing. When they finished their trip, they had set the record of being the fastest to have rowed across the Indian Ocean and having the smallest crew cross the Indian Ocean by rowing.

Nysted has made several trips across oceans and is the first to row across two of the world's seven seas in the same year.

## The Olsen Siblings

In The Guinness Book of World Records 2017, the Olsen siblings from Rituvík on Eysturoy had the highest combined age of twelve living siblings.

To document and prove this record, the twelve siblings, seven brothers and five sisters, had to gather information about themselves which they had relatives and government officials to help them with. This proved challenging because many of them had never received a birth certificate or passport, making the process long and sturdy.

On the 14th of August 2014, it was confirmed that they had reached the high age of *1.025 years and 41 days* combined.

- Magnus Salomon "Maggi" (b. the 30th of October 1920)
- Vensil (b. 8th of October 1921)
- Sára Malena (b. the 20th of February 1923)
- Marin Fredrikka (b. 18th of August 1924)
- Arnholt Sofus (b. the 28th of September 1925)
- Carl Sivar (b. the 25th of January 1928)
- Elly (b. the 14th of February 1930)
- Jaspur (b. the 24th of July 1932)
- Harry (the 3rd of September 1933)
- Mary Elina (b. the 8th of December 1934)
- Amy (b. the 6th of September 1936)
- Arni Kartni (b. the 30th of June 1938)

On the 9th of July 2017, Maggie, the oldest brother, sadly passed away, making their final age count *1.059 years, eight months and 22 days*. This last count has, however, not been confirmed by Guinness.

On the 15th of December 2020, Guinness World Records announced that the D'Cruz family from Pakistan had beaten the record set by the Olsen siblings. Their record was set to *1.042 years and 315 days*, making their combined age some *44 years younger than the final age count for the Olsens*. However, according to the Guinness Book of Records, the D'Cruz family still holds the official record.

## The World's First Underwater Roundabout

In 2020, the sub-sea tunnel Eysturoyartunnilin opened, connecting the two sides of the Skálafjørður fjord in Eysturoy with Tórshavn. This sub-sea tunnel is the third of its kind in the Faroe Islands and the second time Eysturoy and Streymoy have been connected.

Unlike the two previous subsea tunnels, this one has three entrances and a roundabout which connects the three tunnel entrances. In the world, tunnels have been built before that contain a roundabout, but according to World Record Academy, this was the first time a roundabout has ever been built in a subsea tunnel.

The tunnel is generally received as a groundbreaking investment into the Faroese infrastructure, making a better connection between the two largest and most populated areas in the Faroes, though people have been critiquing the high costs of the toll road, which is, however, becoming cheaper as the years pass and the government's debt of building the tunnel is being paid off.

*Picture of tunnel workers celebrating the drill through*

To honour this investment in the infrastructure and to honour the fact that this tunnel is the first of its kind with a roundabout, the roundabout is decorated by artist Tróndur Patursson. The art piece is the silhouettes of people dancing the Faroese chain dance. Also, as an added feature, the prominent musician Jens L. Thomsen, best known for the electronic band Orka, has made a musical piece, which one can tune in on using the car radio, made from mixing the sounds of the tunnel. This track can be heard on the radio channel **FM 97,0**.

# Fun Facts

**Language**

- The Faroe Islands literally means "Sheep Islands."

- The Faroese language, widely spoken by everyone on the islands, is most closely related to Icelandic and the Old Norse language, which does not exist today.

- There are three official languages: Faroese, Danish and Faroese sign language.

- Since June 2017, Faroese sign language has been formally recognised as an official language. However, no school offers lectures in Faroese sign language.

- English is also taught at school and is spoken by most of the population.

- The word *Sjeikur* is Faroese for boyfriend. It derives from Rodolph Valentino's movie *The Sheik* from 1920, which became so popular that the word Sheik became synonymous with the word boyfriend. Today "sjeikur" is the most commonly used word for boyfriend.

- In Faroese, the word *danga* is like a beaten-up rotten ship. The word is said to derive from when Faroese fishermen first came to England to buy used schooners for the Faroese fishing fleet. Since they didn't know English at that time, they bought vessels with signs reading "danger" on them.

- In Faroese, there are 37 words for fog and 140 words for rain.

- The alphabet contains sex letters that aren't found in English, which are Á, Í, Ó, Æ, Ø and Ð, plus an additional three combined letters, which, in the Faroese alphabet, are perceived letters in and of themselves; Ei, Ey, and Oy.

- The alphabet does not include the letters C, X and Z.

- In the Faculty of Faroese Language and Litterature at the University of the Faroe Islands, there is a safe which contains every word within the Faroese language. These words were collected around the islands around the same time as the university was established. Ever since new words have been added after being accepted by the Faroese Language Council.

- The most common word for being dull is "býttur." Directly translated, it means "being switched," which stems from the old superstitious belief of the hidden people, who were believed to be a kind of elves who lived in a parallel society which was not accessible by people. People believed that dull people had been switched as infants with the children of the hidden people. This same belief can also be found in Icelandic superstition.

- In Danish, it is often stated that other languages do not have a word for the Danish word *hygge*. This is false because this word also exists in Faroese and is called *hugni*.

- Many words in English have a Norn origin (the language of the Vikings), which highly resembles modern Faroese and modern Icelandic. Examples of such words are: *father, mother, husband, knife, crook, loan, egg, steak, freckle, window, ill, die, rotten, skill,* and many others, including pronounces such as *they* and *their*.

## Culture

- The national bird is not the puffin. It's the oystercatcher.

- Since the 14th of December 2021, the traditional Faroese clinker boat has been included in the UNESCO List of Intangible Cultural Heritage of Humanity.

- It is often said that the Faroe Islands have 70.000 sheep. According to the Agricultural Agency, Búnaðarstovan, and the Environment Agency, Umhvørvisstovan, this number is just an estimation because there has never been a sheep counting. The estimation is based on how many sheep are allowed on all the different land properties around the islands and does not consider the young sheep. How many sheep there are is unknown.

- The island of Koltur is the only national park there is. It became a national park in 2018 and will serve as a nature reserve and research station. Here the plan is to remove all grazing animals so that researchers can investigate the flora in its natural habitat without animal interference.

- In 2016, National Geographic Traveler elected the Faroe Islands as the most appealing island destination from a selected list of archipelagos.

- In 2021, the Faroe Islands were chosen as 1 of the 30 best places to travel by Lonely Planet.

- Even though Ólavsøka, which is held annually on the 28. - 29. July is often seen as a national holiday, but the Faroe Islands doesn't technically have one.

- Although Ólavsøka is not technically a Faroese national day, in March 2016, the Danish government decided to make Ólavsøka a Danish flag-flying day, even though the Faroese flag day is on 25 March. The decision to choose Ólavsøka over the official flag day in the Faroe Islands caused great surprise among several Danish and Faroese politicians. Still, the decision was made anyway, and Denmark made Ólavsøka an official flag day in Denmark. When Flag Day was to be celebrated in Denmark on 29 July 2016, and all Danish public institutions had to raise the flag, it turned out to be the wrong flag that was raised on the flagpoles - the colours had been switched around. In 2018, the correct flag was raised, but this was on the wrong date, 29 June. This happened again on the same date in 2020 and 2021.

- Even though *Tú Alfagra Land Mítt* (Thou Fairest Land of Mine) is best known as the national anthem, it technically isn't, as it isn't stated in any legislation. In some places, this song isn't recognised as the national anthem; instead, they claim another song to be the anthem which is called *Boðar Tú Til Allar Tjóðir* (When You Send Word to all Nations).

- The Faroese chain dance was common in Europe, but this tradition has vanished in all other European countries. The chain dance is still alive in the Faroes and is being danced to a chanting called kvæði.

- In September 1990, the Faroese football team won their first tournament game versus Austria, resulting in a great Faroese celebration.

- Gunnar Nielsen, a defender for Motherwell in Scotland, is the only footballer from the island to have participated in the Premier League.

- Faroese superstition says many mythical beings live in the mountains and at sea. Amongst these creatures are giants, trolls, kelpies, pixies, selkies, mermaids and mermen, sea ghosts, regular ghosts and hidden people, which are elfish people living in a parallel society.

- In Skopun, there is the world's second-largest mailbox. According to the Guinness Book of World Records, it was the world's most oversized mailbox when it was built.

- Actor James McAvoy (b. 1979) is the only internationally recognised actor to have played in two different movie sets set in the Faroe Islands: the movie Submergence (2017) and the series His Dark Materials (2019 - 2022).

- The largest movie set ever filmed in the Faroe Islands is the James Bond movie, No Time to Die (2021).

- Disney's Peter Pan & Wendy (2023) was the second largest movie.

## History

- Irish monks were the first people known to have settled on the Faroe Islands. This is supported by archaeological excavations, document analysis from British documents and placenames, which indicate Irish presence. Examples of placenames are Vestmanna, meaning West Men, and Saksun, meaning Saxon and Mykines, which combines the Celtic words Muk and Innis, which translates into Colt Isle.

- Archaeological excavations have also shown that people lived on the islands in the year 300 though nothing is known of those people.

- Norwegian Vikings first arrived around the year 800.

- Around the Viking settlement, Frisians also arrived in Suðuroy. They lived in a parallel society and kept to themselves on the southern part of the southernmost island. When the Black Plague struck the Faroes, all the Frisians died except for two, who married other Faroese people.

- The Faroese parliament, Løgtingið, is among the oldest parliaments. It was used for the first time in 825.

- Sverrir Sigurðsson, King of Norway (b. 1177 - d. 1202), was born and raised in Kirkjubø.

- The farmhouse in Kirkjubø is one of the oldest wooden houses in the world, which is still in use. Its oldest parts were built around the year 1350.

- The Black Plague struck in 1349, killing off one-third of the population.

- The potato was first mentioned in writing in Vestmanna in 1686, 51 years before Denmark and 64 years before Norway.

- From 1500 to 1700, pirate invasions hit the Faroe Islands hard. The pirates were primarily from France and Turkey.

- Niels Ryberg Finsen (b. 1860 - d. 1904) was a Faroese doctor who received the Nobel Prize in 1903 for his medical contribution to treating diseases with concentrated light radiation, especially lupus vulgaris (tuberculosis on the skin).

- The Faroe Islands is the country in the world with the most Nobel Prize winners per capita.

- In 1849, Napoleon Bonaparte was said to have visited the islands on his journey in the North Atlantic. This has not been confirmed. However, the French fleet did sail the North Atlantic during this time, and Napoleon Bonaparte did take part in that voyage.

- Runic stones have been found nationwide, the most famous being the Fámjin Stone, the Kirkjubø Stone and the Sandavágur Stone. These are the three most significant ones, though another stone is believed to hold significance: the Froðba Stone. It was found in the mid-1800s and is currently kept in the National Museum in Denmark. Runes have also been carved into wood, which is kept in the National Museum in Tórshavn.

- During World War II, the Faroe Islands were occupied by Brittain. The islands were flooded with British soldiers, and at one point, approximately 8.000 British soldiers were staying there.

- During the war, 205 Faroese fishermen lost their lives at sea. This is the highest death rate per capita during the war.

- In 1992, the Faroe Islands hit a great economic depression. Over 10% of the entire population left the country and 25% of those who remained were unemployed.

## Politics

- Even though Denmark is part of the European Union, the Faroe Islands are not.

- Because the island is not part of the European Union, all trade is handled by bilateral agreements.

- In 2013, the European Union boycotted all trade with the Faroe Islands due to overfishing. This was because the Faroe Islands, in a dispute with the United Kingdom, decided to increase fishing in their own waters, as the marcel population had moved from British to Faroese waters. As Denmark was part of the EU, Denmark took part in the boycott. This is the only time that one part of the Danish Kingdom of Realm has boycotted another part within the Realm. The boycott from the European Union resulted in the Faroe Islands increasing their trade with Russia.

- In 1946, the Faroe Islands voted for independence from Denmark. The vote was dismissed because the result wasn't deemed convincing.

- Women had their first vote in 1906 and voted for legislation which banned the use of alcohol.

- Even though they had voted in 1906, women got the official right to vote in 1916, one year later than Denmark and 13 years before women in the United Kingdom.

- In 1993, Marita Petersen, a candidate from the Social Democrats, became the first, and to this day, only female prime minister of the Faroe Islands.

- In 2015, the first openly homosexual MP, Sonja Jógvansdóttir, was elected.

- Since 2017, same-sex marriage has been legal.

- Since 2021, the adoption of children by same-sex female couples has been legalised, while same-sex male couples still haven't gotten this right.

- The abortion law from 1956 strictly prohibits abortions. This is an ongoing debate that has divided the two opposing sides.

- In 1988, FIFA was the first international association to recognise the Faroe Islands as full members. This was the only international association that the Faroe Islands took part in independent from Denmark until 2021, when the National Union of Faroese Students,

Meginfelag Føroyskra Studenta, entered the European Students' Union as full member.

## Society

- The Gross Domestic Product growth of the Faroe Islands is among the world's highest.

- About 80% of the population is part of the Faroese Lutheran Church, while another 10% are affiliated with the Christian Brethren movement. The other 10% are either atheists or subscribe to other religions.

- There are approximately 245 yearly marriages and 70 divorces yearly. Two-thirds of the marriages are within the State Church.

- The Faroese society is highly digitalised, and many public services are available on an app called Talgildu Føroyar, translated: Digitalised Faroes. This app is connected to people's citizen numbers and allows people to apply for student grants, pensions, funds, etc. They can also register themselves when they move from one municipality to another and when they need to sign their children up for kindergartens. Also, through this app, everyone even has their ancestry tree available.

- Healthcare is free. Dental care is not.

- The average life expectancy is 83,9 years (numbers from 2021); for women, it's 85,6, and for men, it's 82,1 years.

- Education is free, and students receive a monthly student grant for studying.

- On a yearly average, Faroese people consume 6,7 litres of pure alcohol and 59,3 litres of beer (numbers from 2021).

- Statistics of every whale hunt date back to 1584, making it the oldest unbroken statistic from any hunted animal in the world.

- Criminal rates are among the world's lowest, and the Faroe Islands have no prisons.

- Many Faroe Islanders do not use door keys and do not lock doors, as there is close to no theft.

- Alcohol is legal on all islands except for Lítla Dímun. This is because of the steep mountainsides that make intoxication dangerous.

- Funningur is among the oldest settlements in the Faroe Islands and was settled around 825 which makes it more than three times older than the United States of America.

- During the official Church holidays, drinking or dancing from 9 am to 4 pm is illegal.

- During the church holidays, Maundy Thursday (also known as Holy Thursday) and Good Friday, drinking or dancing is illegal. The dates for these church holidays vary but are always between March 19th and April 22nd.

## Industry

- Bakkafrost is a salmon factory. It is the largest fish farming factory and the largest private employer in the Faroe Islands. It is also the third-largest fish farming company in the world.

- The fishing industry contributes to nearly all sales and half of the country's GDP. Tourism is the country's second-largest industry.

- In 2017, the restaurant KOKS received its first Michelin star; in 2019, it was awarded yet another Michelin star.

- In 2022, the two sister restaurants to KOKS, RÆST and ROKS, entered the Michelin Guide.

- In 2017, the tourist bureau, Visit Faroe Islands was awarded the Cannes Award for their campaign Sheep View. Sheep View was an attempt to get Google's attention and to have Google Street View to the Faroe Islands. In Sheep View, panoramic cameras were fitted on sheep's backs and set loose to roam the mountainsides. The sheep could then be trailed like with Street View. One addition to the campaign was a camera which was placed onto a wheelbarrow in the village of Bø. Those who tried Sheep View could "walk" where the wheelbarrow had been. The campaign resulted in Google Street View being available in the Faroe Islands.

- In 2018, Visit Faroe Islands received another award for the campaign Faroe Islands Translate. Again, this campaign was to get Google's attention and have Faroese as part of Google Translate. In this campaign, Faroese volunteers translated sentences on video recordings, with sentences open for anyone to suggest.

## Infrastructure

- The Faroe Islands have four subsea tunnels connecting the islands and are the only toll roads in the Faroes. These are:

    - *Vágatunnilin* (2002), which connects Vágar and Streymoy.

    - *Norðoyartunnilin* (2005), which connects Borðoy and Eysturoy

    - *Eysturoyartunnilin* (2020), which connects Eysturoy and Streymoy. This tunnel is the world's first subsea tunnel to have its own roundabout and three openings. The *við Streymin* bridge also connects the two islands since 1973.

    - *Sandoyartunnilin* (2023), which connects Streymoy and Sandoy.

- The government plans to build yet another tunnel that connects Sandoy and Suðuroy, the southernmost island. It is expected to be built by the year 2030.

- The subsea tunnel, Eysturoyartunnilin, is the first tunnel in the world to have an underwater roundabout.

- There are 21 tunnels in total.

- There are approximately 487 kilometres of road, 41 of which are tunnels and subsea tunnels.

- The Streymin Bridge connects the islands of Streymoy and Eysturoy and is said to be "the world's only bridge crossing the Atlantic Ocean."

- It is often said that only three signal lights are on the Faroes. This is not true. There are ten signal lights in total.

- There is a scenic route marked with a buttercup flower. This route leads to the most scenic roads on the islands.

- For every 1.000 people, there are 520 cars, meaning there are over 25.000 cars on the Faroe Islands.

- Buses are free in Tórshavn and Klaksvík.

- About 50% of all energy comes from renewable energy sources. The goal is to reach 100% by the year 3030.

- Electricity was first introduced in 1921 in Botnur, part of Vágur municipality in Suðuroy.

- A national phone book has been published annually with nearly all the country's phone numbers since the telephone first arrived. With the internet, the use of the phone book saw a decline. When the last edition of the phone book was printed in 2017, it contained the phone number of many politicians, including the personal phone number of the Prime Minister.

- Helicopter rides are part of the routes between some of the smaller islands. They can be booked for a relatively small fee when on the route.

- 98% of households have wireless internet.

- High-speed internet has been available on all 18 islands since 3G. Since 2022, the 5G network has had 100% geographic coverage and coverage at sea, spanning 120 kilometres in all directions, meaning there is coverage until you reach international waters.

- A speed test conducted in March 2023, using 5G, was the fasted measured connection ever recorded in Europe.

- Because of the fast internet connection, the Faroese telecom, Føroya Tele, will provide internet to SaxaVord, the UK Space Port, in the Shetland Islands.

## Geography

- The Faroe Islands archipelago is made of 18 islands. Because of their elongated shape, you can never be farther than 5km from the ocean.

- The islands are made from volcanic eruptions.

- There are only a handful of warm springs ever found in the Faroes. The first discovered, Varmakelda, is believed to have been known since Viking time and is first mentioned in writing in 1673. It was believed that this spring had healing powers. It is approximately 18 degrees Celsius.

- 17 of 18 islands are inhabited, while the 18th island, Lítla Dímun, has not been inhabited since Viking times. Simultaneously Lítla Dímun is the only island that is privately owned.

- Although the Faroe Islands are in the GMT 0 time zone, the westernmost island, Mykines, is partly in GMT -1. This means that Mykines is technically in two time zones. The border between these two time zones exactly hits the stream that runs through the island's only village.

- You can see the Northern Lights in the winter.

- Cape Enniberg is the highest sea cliff in Europe and one of the highest sea cliffs in the world.

- The Faroe Islands have often had all four distinct seasons in a single day.

- The average temperature is 7 degrees Celsius.

- The warmer months of May to August are the best time to visit the Faroe Islands.

- Driftwood that washes up on the Faroese shores is primarily from Siberia, secondly Canada, and thirdly Norway.

## Animals

- The Faroe Islands used to have white-tailed eagles on some high mountain peaks. Some placenames are named after eagles, indicating their residence, and legends tell of tragic incidents where the eagles have taken small children. The last white-tailed eagle was shot in the early 1900s.

- The White Pead Raven, or the White Raven, as the islanders know it, was the same species as the regular black raven that still lives in the Faroes. It only lived in the Faroe Islands; the last raven was seen in 1948 in Nólsoy. However, scientists speculate that the DNA could still be carried with the current breed and hope that the Faroe Islands one day will have the White Raven as one of its local species.

- Frogs were first introduced in Nólsoy in 2002; in 2004, they had their first offspring. Nólsoy is the only island that has frogs.

- There are plenty of seals which, during the summer mornings, can be seen resting on the rocky beaches around the islands. According to the Faroese myth, the seals are people who have committed suicide by throwing themselves into the sea from the high mountainous cliffs or fishermen who have drowned while at sea. From this belief, it is said that on the 6th of January, the seals come to land at midnight, taking off their hides and then taking the shape of people. On this night, they dance until sunrise.

- Drunnhvíti, The European storm petrel, reciedes in Nólsoy, Mykines and on some other islands. Nólsoy is the largest breeding area for this bird species in the world.

- Skúgvur, the Great Skua, recedes in high numbers on the island of Skúvoy, which is the world's largest breeding area for this species. When people first settled on the Faroe Islands, there were so many birds on the island that the island itself was named after them.

- In 1855, Norwegian hares were set loose into the Faroese mountains. They were introduced as a new food resource. When it was introduced, it was brown, but after some 50 years, the hare had adapted to its new surroundings. Now the hare is brown in the summer and grey in the winter.

- Even though the Faroe Islands have legal whale hunts, there is no such thing as a whaling season.

- The Faroe Islands means "Sheep Islands" (plural), and the Scottish island, Soay, where the sheep breed still lives, which is closest related to the original Faroese sheep, means "Sheep Island" (singular).

- Faroese for Albatross is Súlukongur, which means *the King of the Gannets*. This comes from the 1950s when an albatross nested among the gannets in Mykines for some years.

- In 2023 birdwatchers noticed that the gannet had switched eye colour from bright blue to black. It's unclear why this has happened, but since 2021 the gannet has been infected with bird flu which is believed to be the cause of the changed colour.

# RÚNI Í MÚLA

THE OBSCURE AND FUN FACTS OF THE FAROE ISLANDS

# The Unique Travel Guide

The Faroe Islands, brimming with vibrant creativity and innovation, offer diverse cultural experiences in music, art, literature, crafts, design, and gastronomy. Traditions from the Faroe Islands have been preserved while allowing new creative forces to flourish.

Despite centuries of isolation, the Faroe Islands have developed a distinct and rich culture. Because of the relative isolation, access to instruments, tools, and materials was previously very limited. As a result, storytelling, ballads, and the distinctive chain dance play an essential role in Faroese cultural heritage, and singing is deeply rooted in Faroese culture.

Over the last centuries, as the Faroes have become increasingly more connected to the rest of the world, the cultural scene has evolved and grown and is still flourishing.

However, artists in all fields continue to draw inspiration from the riches of Faroese nature and tradition.

In this chapter, I will provide you with the best recommendations on what to see and do during your stay, many of which are amongst the cheapest attractions within the country.

## Art, Music and Culture

The Faroe Islands have a very diverse and vivid cultural scene. Music and the arts are flourishing, and you can see artists in music and the fine arts represented worldwide. Music especially has been very well represented; in television series, videogames and so forth, some musicians have even been signed by labels such as Universal Records.

Why that is, well, that is a question that hasn't been investigated, but if you look at habits and tastes among Faroese youth, it is common to see original paintings in homes, even in the homes of people in the late teenage years.

Music is an essential part of Faroese culture and part of the morning ritual in every public school, where students and teachers sing songs each morning before class. Also, in the olden days, the tradition of chain dance and singing within the Faroese homes has been a natural part of everyday life. Today, this tradition has vanished, but the chain dance and singing of old hymns and ballads have remained a part of the public school curriculum.

Music and art are also part of the curriculum, ensuring that anyone, regardless of their interest, will be introduced to music and art. Also, the music training system is available nationwide, where public school students can be taught an instrument after the demanded classes. Following this, students who wish to pursue a career in music can take an upper-secondary diploma in music, which is inspired by the music conservatory traditions and gives access to most of the world's conservatories. After finishing this diploma, they can continue their studies at the University of the Faroe Islands, offering a Bachelor of Arts program in music production and theory as a Bachelor of Arts program in creative writing.

Through the years, many music contests have been held annually, where participants can win a tour abroad or are given the opportunity to perform at the annual music festivals.

In this section, you will be provided with the most recommended places to visit or experience if you are interested in music, arts or culture.

## The G! festival

The Faroe Islands' most exciting and culturally challenging music festival, always guaranteeing a broad and diverse range of enjoyable musical and cultural elements. The festival is in Syðrugøta, a small village surrounded by high mountain tops and a sandy beach. The festival is typically held in mid-June.

If you're looking for a vibrant musical experience with a surprisingly good atmosphere and the best of what a music experience can offer, the G! Festival is the number one recommendation.

See more at: www.gfestival.fo

## Summertónar

The Composers' and Songwriters' Festival, Summartónar, offers various concerts throughout the summer. The concerts are held around the entire country and in different sceneries; from the heart of Tórshavn to the outer islands such as Svínoy, onboard the old schooner, Norðlýsið, and within the sea caves of Hestur.

If you're looking for a unique experience, it is worth looking at the Summartónar programme.

See more: www.summartonar.fo

## Hoyma: Home Concerts

Hoyma is a concept where concerts are held in people's homes. It is very similar to concepts such as Sofar Sounds and Sofa Concerts, but unlike Sofar Sounds, anyone can buy tickets to the venues. Hoyma is held locally in Syðrugøta, home to the G! festival, and the founders of Hoyma are the same as the founders of the festival.

Concerts are held sporadic throughout the year and are predominately held off-season.

In 2021, Lonely Planet included the Faroe Islands as one of the best destinations on the annual Best in Travel list. The reason for being included on this list was partly because of the Hoyma concerts and Heimablídni (see page 147).

Tickets and information on the venues can be found on the website www.hoyma.fo.

## Museums of Fine Art

You find the National Museum of Art in the heart of Tórshavn, on the outskirts of the central park, with many planted trees. This museum offers the best of art ever made in the Faroes. With household names such as Sámal J. Mikines and Tróndur Patursson, you can see some of the original paintings that have made these artists famous worldwide.

Address:    Gundadalsvegur 9, Tórshavn
Phone:      (+298) 22 35 79
e-mail:     info@art.fo
Website:    www.art.fo

An alternative visit worth doing is going to the Art Gallery on Sandur, Sandoy, a private collection donated to the village by art collector Sofus Olsen, who also paid for the impressive gallery building. This museum is on the same level as the national museum, showcasing many impressive works by some of the most prominent Faroese artists.

Address:    Áarbøur 11, Sandur
Phone:      (+298) 21 19 24
e-mail:     info@listasavnid.fo
Website:    www.listasavnid.fo

## Heystfagnaður and Sjómannadagar

Each fall in Eiði, the village hosts a local festival focusing on agriculture and farming. Here, people are competing with performing tasks from the traditional Faroese way of life such as slaughtering a sheep or seeing who can lift a sack of potatoes the longest. Many old traditions are on display for anyone to enjoy.

For many, the Heystfagnaður festival is perceived as being a counter-culture to modern life in Tórshavn, though the festival is trendy for people from Tórshavn.

During the festival, there is an animal zoo with domestic animals, you can buy roots and vegetables grown locally, the local museums and the church are open, and the boat houses are all filled with different activities; for the grownups, beer is served, and there are many activities for children.

Heystfagnaður is typically held mid-October, and you can keep yourself orientated by following their Facebook page "Heystfagnaður á Eiði".

Another similar village festival is Sjómannadagar, held annually in Klaksvík in August. Much like the Heystfagnaður, Sjómannadagar is a local village festival focusing on fisheries and everything related to fisheries.

## Ólavsøka

Ólavsøka is the largest town festival of the year, and many perceive it to be the Faroese national holiday. It has often been called such in books and articles about the Faroe Islands and many in fact sheets about the Faroe Islands the Ólavsøka festival is said to be the Faroese National Holiday.

But, even though this isn't true, the Ólavsøka festival is the largest annual festival, and it is also during this festival that the Løgting has its formal annual assembly.

On Ólavsøka, the streets of Tórshavn are brimming with people from all over the country, and during this season, many tourists can also be seen.

If you wish to visit Tórshavn during Ólavsøka, you must secure your accommodation beforehand since it can be hard to get accommodation during these days.

## The Knitting Festival

Each year around April the knitting festival, Bindifestivalurin, is held in Fuglafjørður. This is a significant event, mainly focusing on knitting, spinning, and anything made from wool, and the festival contains lecturers, hiking trips and a wide span of workshops. The festival itself is arranged by locals and is tied to the local home industry, which has a shop in one of the village's old buildings and is run by volunteer workers.

The festival attracts people from the Faroes and has visitors from all over the world, many of whom either participate or hold the workshops and lectures.

The festival is usually held over three days, and visitors can buy single-day tickets or tickets for the whole festival.

See dates, prices and more: www.bindifestival.com

## Heimavirki: Home-Made Goods

Heimavirki translates into Home Industry and is a well-known way of buying and selling Faroese-made products such as sweaters and other home-produced goods. These craft shops are run by volunteer workers, local to the different areas, and usually, these workers are also some of the producers of the products sold in these shops.

**Føroya Heimavirkisfelag**
Address: Niels Finsens Gøta 7, Tórshavn

**Lávusarhús**
Address: Á bakka 2, Leirvík

**Norðoya Heimavirki**
Address: Biskupsgøta 11, Klaksvík

**Ribarhús & Piddasahandil**
Address: Í støð 14, Fuglafjørður

**Suðuroyar Heimavirki**
Address: Vágsvegur 47, Vágur

# History and Historic Sites

Despite only a little more than a thousand years and lacking written historical documents, the Faroe Islands are not poor in their history.

Historic houses have been preserved throughout the country, and archaeological excavations have shown old settlements throughout many villages.

In many villages, statues have been put up that tell of the many myths that are told locally. You can find the Selkie in Mikladalur, the Nix in Lake Leitisvatn, the Merman in Elduvík and Fuglafjørður and the Shepherd of Sondum in Miðvágur.

The most historical places are Kirkjubø, Tinganes in Tórshavn, the old farm of Hoyvík, the old Fort in Tórshavn, and the World War II ruins that are scattered around, especially on the island of Vágar.

There are also a handful of abandoned villages you can visit by hiking. A list of the villages are also included in this chapter.

## Historical Museums

A great way of experiencing the Faroe Islands is by visiting the museums. Here are a few recommendations that are worth a visit and, perhaps, more interesting than other museums you can also find across the country.

## The National Museum

Tjóðsavnið, or the National Museum, has a permanent and an open-air exhibition with different interchangeable instalments. Here you can get a glimpse of the history and culture of the Faroe Islands and its nature.

You can expect to see old Faroese clothing, the traditional Faroese clinker boat, silver coins and other findings from archaeological excavations, stuffed examples of extinct animal species, old photos, stones and gems from nature and much more.

Address: Brekkutún 6, Hoyvík
Phone: (+298) 31 80 76
e-mail: savn@savn.fo
Website: www.tjodsavnid.fo

## SagaMuseum

SagaMuseum in Vestmanna is a wax museum that evolves around the history and sagas of the Faroe Islands. In the museum, several realistic-looking wax figures are placed in surroundings that either reference places and surroundings from history or exact copies of historical places around the islands. The museum visit is a virtual tour through time, from the Viking Age until today, and it is a great introduction to the history of the Faroe Islands as told through the Færeyinga Saga, myth and documented history.

Museum visitors can get tickets to the boat tour to the Vestmanna Bird Cliffs for a reduced price and vice versa.

Address:     Fjarðavegur 2, Vestmanna
Phone:       (+298) 47 15 00
e-mail:      touristinfo@olivant.fo
website:     www.visit-vestmanna.com


**The War Museum**

By the airport in Vágar, you can find the World War II museum. It is a museum located in an old Military building, used by the British soldiers in the area where there was the most military activity.

The museum collects artefacts from the war, and presentations and stories are often told from the war times.

Address:     Varðagøta 61, Sørvágur
Phone:       (+298) 22 19 40
e-mail:      krigssavnid@ww2.fo
Website:     www.ww2.fo

## Viking settlements

In Leirvík and Kvívík, you can visit some well-preserved ruins that have been dug out in the two villages. Both places are free and open to visitors.

Both settlements are tiny and have described signs about the respective areas and what has been found during the excavations. If you go to Kvívík, you can also enjoy the small cosy village, famous for its tiny houses with grass-covered roofs and the stream that runs through the village.

## How to get there:

When you look out towards the sea, the Kvívík settlement is down by the shore, on the right-hand side. The Leirvík settlement is located in a field above the main road right after you pass the petrol station after arriving through the tunnel.

## Kirkjubø

Arguably one of the most important sites of the Middle Ages, Kirkjubøur is one of the most historic sites of the Faroe Islands. Here, you can see one of the world's oldest wooden houses, the ruined Magnus Cathedral, the oldest church of the Faroes and the cave where the Norwegian king, Sverrir Sigurðsson, is said to have lived.

Visiting Kirkjubø is always a recommendation and can be done with or without a local guide. For the ultimate experience, booking a guide, preferably someone local, is recommended. If you decide to use the local farmer as a guide, it is one of the **cheapest tourist attractions** in the Faroe Islands and **contributes to the farm's economy**.

See more: www.patursson.fo

## Ghosts of Tórshavn: The Lost Commandant

This self-guided tour leads you through the most haunted, historic and scenic places in Tórshavn, and is amongst the cheapest tourist attractions in the Faroe Islands.

The game is a mix between an escape room and geo catching, where you wander through the streets of Tórshavn, solving riddles and cracking codes to progress in the game.

See more: [www.questoapp.com](www.questoapp.com) or by downloading the Questo app on App Store or Google Play. Prices are available on the app.

## Tinganes and Reyn: The Old District of Tórshavn

The oldest and most historic place in Tórshavn is Tinganes and Reyn. The iconic old wooden buildings, many of which have grass roofs, are painted in a traditional Faroese style, and these sites are the cosiest district in town.

Tinganes is where the old Viking assembly was, which back then shared the same name as the Icelandic thing, Altingið, but was later renamed to Løgtingið. On this site, many sentences were made, people were executed and drowned (see page 18 - 21) and new laws were made.

Tinganes was also the trading center during the time of the King's Monopoly Store, and the Danish officials had their main offices there.

In 1673, Tinganes was set on fire, and many of the old houses that used to stand there, burned to the ground. Therefore, many of the buildings that are still standing, have been built in the years after.

Today, Tinganes serves as parliamentary buildings where politicians and public offices are hosted.

## Skansin: The Old Fort

First built in 1580, the old fort, Skansin, is the oldest military instalment on the Faroe Islands, and through time it has served several different purposes; a prison, for protection from private ships and invaders and during World Ward II, it was the main quarters for the British military.

Through time, the fort has been rebuilt and expanded, and initially, it was one of three forts of its kind in Tórshavn. Today, the Skansin Fort is the only fort still standing and serves as a free park area that anyone can visit freely.

## Koltur Island

Second to Lítla Dímun, Koltur is the most isolated island in the Faroes. The old village with stone houses with grass roofs is still standing, and can be visited, should you decide to go. Also, Koltur has a small sandy beach and a modern farmhouse, where the islands' only two residents live.

Koltur is the only national park in the Faroes, and in the near future, all sheep will be removed from the island, letting nature flourish without any animal interference. Additionally, the Faroese government plans on establishing a research station on the island, which will be built in a traditional Faroese way. Also, when the research station is established, Koltur will also be made more accessible as a tourist attraction.

## Áir Whaling Station

In Áir, between Hósvík and Hvalvík, there are many tiny red houses. This used to be a whaling station where industrialised whaling used to take place in the olden days. Now, the station is marked as an industrial heritage site and is part of the National Museum, and you can visit on-site and get a guided tour.

The whaling station is one of three in the world and is the only station still standing in the northern hemisphere.

You can visit the whaling station without payment, but if you wish to tour the site to access the many industrial buildings, you must take the tour.

The whaling station is open from 10 am to 5 pm on Saturdays and Sundays from mid-June to mid-august, and prices for a guided tour.

| | |
|---|---|
| Prices for adults | 80 DKK |
| Prices for students and seniors: | 50 DKK |
| Prices per person in a group of 10 or more: | 50 DKK |

Children have free entry.

## Abandoned villages

Throughout the Faroe Islands, many villages have been abandoned through time. Most of these villages have been demolished because of tragic deaths, where in many cases, all the men from the village have been lost at sea. Since this was before roads were built, they are only accessible by foot.

Skarð, Kunoy
Only accessible with a paid guide. Contact Visit Norðoy to purchase a guided hike.

Blankskáli, Kalsoy
Not accessible by foot.

Múli, Borðoy
Accessible by car.

Víkar, Vágar,
accessible by foot, by walking from Gásadalur. In Gásadalur you can find your route on an information sign.

Slættanes, Vágar
Accessible by foot by heading north from Oyragjógv.

Korndalur, Nólsoy
Easily accessible by foot.

Fámará, Suðuroy
Accessible by car, though the road is very very rough.

Víkarbyrgi, Suðuroy
Accessible by car, narrow road.

Akraberg, Suðuroy
Accessible by car, narrow road.

There are many other abandoned villages, but most of them have been abandoned so many years ago, that all traces from human activity have been lost.

# THE OBSCURE AND FUN FACTS OF THE FAROE ISLANDS

# Restaurants and Dining

Even though everything might seem expensive, fine dining is relatively cheap in the Faroes, and in Tórshavn, there is a wide range of high-end restaurants. Compared with takeaway options, fine dining is not that expensive, and it might be worth considering a finer meal than going to Burger King, etc.

If you prefer a dining experience with fish, steak, high-quality pizza, street-food or traditional Faroese food, Tórshavn has you covered. Most restaurants can be found in the town's centre, and many of the more exclusive restaurants are located in small cottages near Tinganes, which only adds to the authentic experience.

Though it can be harder to find a good quality meal in the rural areas, there are a few places worth a visit, some of whom are at least of the same quality as the high-end restaurants in the capital.

In this section, you will have a list of recommended dining places, with a description of what each place has to offer.

## Heimablídni: Dining in Faroese Homes

The most authentic food experience you can have while visiting the Faroe Islands is to dine with the concept of Heimablídni, home hospitality.

A concept that has proven increasingly popular is the home dining concept Heimablídni. With this concept, locals invite people to dine in their homes with food the hosts have prepared. There are many such places where you can eat, and the food served is as varied and authentic as the hosts themselves and the homes they live in. Because this concept is held in people's homes and by the homeowners, different offers aren't always available, but

A list of places to dine can be found on www.eatlocal.fo, and you can book your reservation there.

Additionally, there is another place where you can eat in the same manner, though this place isn't listed on the before mentioned website.

**Karlsá Heimablídni**, in Klaksvík, makes pizza like no other. They have a separate little shed where guests can eat and have private time, and pizza is served ad-libitum.

Address:     Karlsvegur 6, Klaksvík
Phone:       (+298) 22 44 34
e-mail:      karlsa@karlsa.fo

## ROKS and RÆST

The two restaurants, ROKS and RÆST, are sister restaurants to the famous Faroese restaurant KOKS which has been awarded two Michelin stars. Since KOKS moved to Greenland a few years ago, ROKS and RÆST have been included in the Micheline Guide.

Situated in small cottage-like houses in the old part of Tórshavn, these two restaurants serve very high-quality meals in a cosy environment.

Suppose you'd like to try a modern take on traditional Faroese fermented food. In that case, RÆST is the place for you, and if you'd like to try food that has been caught and harvested locally but that hasn't been part of the traditional Faroese cuisine, such as Faroese lobsters and sea urchins, then ROKS is the place for you.

Either way, both restaurants are well worth a visit, which the Michelin Guide also suggests, and both restaurants serve the best wine you can find on the Faroe Islands.

| | |
|---|---|
| RÆST's address: | Gongin 8, Tórshavn |
| ROKS's address: | Gongin 5, Tórshavn |
| See more at: | www.raest.fo and www.roks.fo |

## Fiskastykkið

In Miðvágur, the restaurant Fiskastykki resides in some old factory buildings used to dry fish. Fiskastykki is the Faroese word for the outdoor area where people used to sun dry fish before piling them up in the warehouses.

Today, these surroundings host a luxurious and cosy café, serving seafood from arguably the best and freshest ingredients.

Address:     Úti á Bakka 12, Sandavágur
Phone:       (+298) 25 06 00
Website:     www.fiskastykkid.fo

**Restaurant Muntra**

In Fuglafjørður, there is a restaurant which serves a wide range of meals. The restaurant has open every day year-round between 12 am to 10 pm but is typically closed in January and February.

The food from this restaurant isn't trying to impress. Still, it relies on a solid traditional way of cooking, with over 40 years of experience and with regular customers since the restaurant first opened.

Restaurant Muntra is most famous for its fish soup, made from dried fish heads delivered from a drying factory in the neighbouring village of Leirvík. These fishheads give an intense aroma and a tasty fish flavour, which you cannot find anywhere else on the Faroe Islands.

Address:     Toftagøta 1 A, Fuglafjørður
Phone:       (+298) 44 40 81

## Vegetarian and Vegan options

Finding vegetarian or vegan restaurants in the Faroe Islands can be challenging, but you can always ask if they serve anything vegan at any restaurant. But, there are some places where they do serve vegan or vegetarian dishes. Here is a list:

- Sirkus, Tórshavn
- Fiskastykkið, Vágar
- Café Fríða, Klaksvík
- Kafe Umami, Tórshavn
- Suppugarðurin, Tórshavn
- Etika Sushi, Tórshavn
- Systrar, Tórshavn
- Bitin, Tórshavn

Additionally, Burger King and Sunset Boulevard have vegetarian options.

Also, most supermarkets have vegan and vegetarian options, if you prefer preparing your own food.

## Other recommended dining experiences

In Tórshavn:

- The Tarv, *steakhouse*
- Áarstova, *steakhouse*
- Barbara Fishhouse, *fish restaurant*
- Skeiva Pakkhús, *Italian food*
- Etika, *sushi*
- Suppugarðurin, *traditional Japanese ramen*
- Reyðleyk, *pizza*
- Haps, *burger joint*
- Geisha, *grill buffet*

Outside Tórshavn:

- Amarant, *bakery and pizza*, Klaksvík
- Rose's Café, *restaurant*, Ljósá

Both in and outside Tórshavn, it's worth to keep an eye out for food trucks, as this is the only way street-food is being served. This is, however, only during the summertime, though some food trucks can be seen in the early spring to late fall.

## Distilleries and Breweries

In recent years, the Faroe Islands have seen a significant expansion of new alcohol products. This happened after the law on alcohol from 1992 was made less restrictive in 2011, making it legal to produce spirits with an alcohol limit of up to 60 % alcohol. Before this change, the law prohibited producing alcohol above 5,8 % alcohol which is why many traditional Faroese beers have that alcohol percentage. Also, until a few years prior, producers weren't allowed to use cans but had to use bottles, making the production and recycling process more expensive.

In the years before the 2011 change, people from the restaurant and hospitality business and people from the breweries advocated for a less restricted regulation so that it could be made possible to produce alcohol with the same alcohol percentage as other imported products that were already legal and selling in the monopoly store for alcohol. But, at that time, the Faroese politicians didn't seem to respond with new legislation – at least not quickly enough – because in 2008, DISM, the first "Faroese distillery", was established.

Even though DISM is a distillery founded by Faroese people, they have not and never had their distillery in the Faroe Islands; instead, the production is in Iceland and Denmark. But DISM insisted on making a Faroese product, so they started exporting fresh Faroese water to these countries, distilling their products and importing it back to the Faroes. In that way, one might consider DISM an authentic Faroese distillery, though they have never had their products made in the Faroes.

The exporting of water to distil, only to import it again as alcohol, made the people wonder about the law, and soon a heated debate started on softening the restrictive alcohol law from 1992, and from there, the 2011 changes were eventually made.

The law has seen many changes in its time, and in recent years it has only become less and less restrictive. But the changes haven't always been easily made. Whenever a coalition wishes to change the law on alcohol, it stirs an extensive debate because alcohol is a sore topic that tends to divide politicians.

The reason for this divisive topic is highly connected to the social problems that came from the extensive use of alcohol before the 1992 law. Back then, there was a shipping system where alcohol was ordered through Denmark. People could order a maximum amount of litres quarterly through the system, divided between wine and strong liquor, while beer was not part of this system.

This had many people ordering as much as they could, and oftentimes, when three months had gone, and they could order again, they had already drunk all they had gotten with the previous order.

It has been speculated that people were paranoid about not having enough to drink, so they always maxed out their "alcohol card". But the social problems of binge drinking go way back in history – perhaps further back than people seem to recognise.

In 1271 the Norwegian king introduced the Monopoly Store, which all trade to and from the Faroe Islands had to go through. This system was in place when the Faroe Islands were under Norwegian rule. When the Faroe Islands became part of the Danish kingdom, the monopoly store continued similarly, with all trades connected to the Danish king. But, in 1855, the monopoly store was demolished, and this was the first time in 584 years that the Faroe Islands had free trade.

With the dissolution of the monopoly store, all trade became free, and all goods could be traded freely, including alcohol. For some years, alcohol abuse became a growing problem, and in 1860 a new law was introduced that defined who could serve and sell alcohol, and taxes were also imposed on both selling and serving to reduce consumption and demarcate the places where it was served. But the Faroe Islands were undergoing major societal development, and although attempts were made to limit alcohol consumption, alcohol abuse still became a growing societal problem. This led to associations being formed around the country that distanced themselves from alcohol, the so-called abstinence associations. In these associations, many women became active and highly involved. In 1906 they demanded that alcohol should be banned by law. This came to a referendum in 1907 when women had the right to vote for the first time. The result was that alcohol production was banned.

Breweries could still continue making beer with a maximum alcohol limit of 4,6 %, but distilling was made illegal. Clubs and pubs could also continue serving alcohol until 1923, when was banned. People could, however, order alcohol from abroad, which were orders they could quarter annually. In

1928 the law became even more restrictive when the right to buy alcohol was intertwined with the tax-paying system. With this law, you could only buy alcohol if you had paid off all your taxes.

In 1936 a new alcohol law was proposed. The idea was to introduce a Faroese monopoly store, which handled all alcohol trade. But people still remembered how things were when alcohol was a free trade product, and the law proposal fell and would leave the political discussions for many years. A similar proposal was put forth in 1973 and was accepted by the then-ruling government, though it had to go through a referendum before it could go into action. The referendum was held, and once again, the proposal was rejected.

In 1980 the strong "Giraffe" and "Elephant" beers were banned, and the alcohol limit of 4,6 % was increased to 5,8 %. This was the first time since the alcohol ban in 1907 that the law was liberalised.

In 1991 the proposal of having a monopoly store for alcohol was reintroduced, with an extensive hearing process with all of society's relevant stakeholders. Once again, it stirred an extensive debate. But on the 10th of March 1992, the law was accepted, and the monopoly store, Rúsan, was established.

Since the monopoly store, the government has kept statistics on alcohol consumption. As it turns out, each time the law has been made less restrictive, and as the monopoly store has increased its service of guiding the consumers in their choice of alcohol, the statistics of alcohol consumption per capita have decreased.

## Faer Isle Distillery

With its distillery and visitor centre located in Vestmanna and its warehouse (still under construction) in the mountains between Vestmanna and Kvívík, the Faer Isle Distillery is amongst the world's youngest Whisky distilleries. Though the distillery was only founded in 2019, it produces several handcrafted, high-quality spirits using local ingredients, such as herbs, seaweed, clear mountain water and water from a subsea tunnel. The Faroese climate makes for ideal whisky maturation in the wet and salty wind.

The Distillery Tour is amongst the **cheapest tourist attractions in the Faroe Islands** and can be booked by phone or e-mail:

Phone: (+298) 77 90 00
e-mail: info@faer.fo
Website: www.faer.io
Address: Fjarðavegur 3, Vestmanna

## Føroya Bjór Brewery and Einar's Distillery

Founded in 1888, Føroya Bjór is the oldest still-running Faroese brewery, which makes a wide selection of products but is most famous for its traditional lagers, many of whom have won prizes for their high quality. The brewery is family owned and is run by the family's third generation. In recent years, the brewery has introduced soft drinks and alcohol-free beer and has also expanded with a distillery named Einar's Distillery after the current owner of Føroya Bjórr, Einar Waag.

Guided tours to the brewery and distillery can be booked by phone or e-mail:

Phone:     (+298) 47 54 54
E-mail:    fb@foroyabjor.fo
Website:   www.bjor.fo and www.einarsdistillery.fo
Address:   Klakksvíksvegur 19, Klaksvík

## Okkara Brewery

As a micro-brewery focusing on high-quality hand-crafted beers, Okkara was the main competitor to Føroya Bjór until 2020, when Føroya Bjór bought it. But even though the brewery was bought, the two breweries have been kept separate, focusing on different styles of beers for the Faroese market.

When founded in 2006, Okkara presented a wide range of new types of beer that had never been brewed in the Faroes before. Some types of beer have been produced and developed in collaboration with the Danish brewery Mikkeler, which also focuses on craft beer.

Phone: (+298) 31 10 30
e-mail: okkar@okkara.fo
website: www.okkara.fo
Address: Uppi á Heiðum 1, Velbastaður

## Biskupskelda Brewery

With a vision of bringing life to old tales from the Faroese myth, the microbrewery Biskupskelda makes its beer with inspiration from old and local folk tales.

It was founded in 2021 in Vágur, Suðuroy, and as of 2022, it has ten different types of beer, five of which can be bought at the Monopoly store, while the other five can only be bought at the brewery.

The brewing started in rented facilities, but in 2022 the brewery bought a historic building which in the future will serve as their primary production building and visitor centre. But, until the building is finished, Biskupskelda offers guided beer walks in the village of Vágur and hikes out in nature. If you wish to visit the brewery, you have to do so by e-mail.

| | |
|---|---|
| e-mail: | biskupskelda@gmail.com |
| website: | www.biskupskelda.fo |
| Address: | Vágsvegur 107B, Vágur |

## OY Brewpub and Take-away

With its combined brewpub and takeaway concept in the same factory building where the beer is brewed, OY is arguably the hippest of all the breweries. You can book a tour through the brewery, have a meal, or just go for a casual pint at their site. On weekends, they often host concerts and other events, such as stand-up comedy.

Oy was founded in 2021 by Faroese beer enthusiasts with experience from Okkara and people from the restaurant and hospitality business.

Beers from OY can be bought at the Monopoly store, but if you visit their site, many more options are kept on tap. And a visit to the brewery is worth a visit.

| | |
|---|---|
| Phone: | (+298) 78 22 00 |
| e-mail: | oy@oy.fo |
| website: | www.oy.fo |
| Address: | Falkavegur 4, Tórshavn |

## Well-known Gems in Nature

In the last 10 years or so, tourism has been booming in the Faroe Islands, attracting television and advertising companies to make commercials on many of the sites, and travel agencies not only in the Faroes, but also in other countries, have been advertising using many of these sites. Because of this, these areas have seen an increasing amount of tourists which are visiting all year around.

Some places have become so popular, that it has damaged the grass and many of the old walking paths, some of whom are hundreds, perhaps thousands of years old. But in reaction to the stressed nature, the Faroese authorities in collaboration with the national tourist bureau, Visit Faroe Islands, have made walking paths to reduce the said stress.

It is, therefore, of most importance that anyone visiting any of these places stick to the paths marked on the trails and that they respect all the signs that have been put up. If not, it can harm the natural area, birdlife and such.

## The Lake Above the Ocean

One of the most visited tourist attractions and one of the most iconic sceneries in the Faroe Islands is, without a doubt, the site at Trælanípa. Trælanípa is the name of the cliffs that reside outside Lake Leitisvatn, best known as the lake above the sea.

It is only a five minutes drive from the airport in Vágar and a 30-minute walk from where you park your car. However, visiting this site demands a fee of **200 DKK**, and with an additional **250 DKK**, you can get a guide to show you around which is the recommended way to go.

## Múlafossur

In this scenic area, with the waterfall falling directly into the Atlantic Ocean and the small quiet village of Gásadalur resting above, you can take one of the Faroe Islands' best pictures on your travels.

This site is the most visited in the Faroes and has been part of many commercials worldwide.

The waterfall is only a ten-minute drive from the Airport in Vágar and is accessible by a short walk from the main road.

If you go to Gásadalur, signs will lead you to it.

## The Giant and the Hag

The two mythical sea stacks, the Giant and the Hag, stand on the sea below the high cliffs, frozen in stone in a failed attempt to pull the Faroe Islands to Iceland. According to legend, they couldn't pull the Faroe Islands all the way to Iceland before the sun rose, turning them into stone.

These sea stacks are probably one of the most famous folktales from the Faroes and can be seen from the village Tjørnuvík or from the narrow road between Eiði and Gjógv (see the Buttercup routes).

If you decide to drive on this Buttercup Route, you should stop by the telescope, where you can investigate them further.

## Saksun and Saksun Beach

Saksun is a small village known for its beautiful natural surroundings. It has often been compared with the Shire from the Lord of the Rings, and understandably so. In Saksun, you can visit the local church, and near the church there are many traditional old houses. But, if you decide to go to this part of the village, please respect the resident's privacy, since these are private homes, and do not look in through the windows.

If you are up for a walk, the trip out on Saksun beach is a short but scenic 20-minute hike.

To go to the beach, you must pay 75 DKK per person to get through a gate, which you can only pay using a credit card.

You can drive to Saksun by car, and there, it is easy to find both the walking trails, the old village and the church.

## Kallur Lighthouse

Not only is this one of the most beautiful places in the Faroe Islands, but it is also relatively inaccessible. Firstly, the Kallur Lighthouse is out on the island Kalsoy, which isn't connected to the main islands, and secondly, it is a steep and long walk from the village Trøllanes. At any measures, this must be considered a hard climb.

It is here that the scenes from the James Bond movie No Time to Die were shot, and where we got the infamous scene, where Agent 007 dies. In his remembrance, the farmer who owns this land has raised a mock tomb-stone, which you can read about in the section about Cinemaography in this book.

## Tjørnuvík Beach and Village

One of the most visited places on Streymoy is the northernmost village, Tjørnuvík. It is a small and cosy old village with many wooden houses with grass roofs. The village itself is surrounded by tall and impressive mountains, with a large sandy beach, from where you can see the Giant and the Hag.

If you decide to go to Tjørnuvík, know that the road is very narrow and that it follows a steep mountain side which is known for many landslides. The risk of landslides is highest when the rain is pouring, especially if it's after a dry season.

If you feel adventurous, and you feel comfortable in the cold wavy water, then you should consider looking up Faroe Islands

Surf Guide, which is a local surfing company where you can rent surfing gear and boards. If you haven't tried surfing before, surfing lessons are also available.

See more at [www.FaroeIslandsSurfGuide.com](www.FaroeIslandsSurfGuide.com) or get in touch by calling (+298) 25 88 98.

You can also try to go by the Surf Shack that is located by the beach and see if you can book a lesson in person.

# Hidden Gems in Nature

Many sites in the Faroes are free from tourists, and very few locals generally visit these places. These gems usually are not commercialised by any tourist agencies but are free to visit. If you decide to go, please respect the owners of the land.

It can be quide difficult finding some of these places, but with help of your mobile phone and the Internet, you'll be able to find them easily. But, many of these places are not visible on apps such as Google Maps. Therefore, you must take notice to the village names, which you can then search for using your device.

THE OBSCURE AND FUN FACTS OF THE FAROE ISLANDS

## The Hidden Beach near Bøur

When you're driving between the villages Bø and Gásadalur in Vágar, there is a sandy beach hidden down by the shore in a gorge called Salgjógv. The high rock walls create shelter from the wind, and therefore, during the summer, it gets very hot on this beach.

## How to get there:

The beach is located right between Bø and the tunnel opening leading to Gásadalur. It can be hard to find, but if you aim for a large skerry visible from the road above (the skerry is so prominent that you won't miss it) and head down towards it, you'll find the hidden beach by heading towards Bø.

Oftentimes, locals go to the beach by boat, but you can also get there by foot. But this is only when the tide is low because when the tide is high, the way of entry is flooded.

You cannot go without asking permission first, which you can do by contacting Visit Vágar.

## Vatndalsvatn: The Heart-shaped Lake

One of the most "Instagram-worthy" places to visit is the heart-shaped lake, Vatndalsvatn. The lake is situated in the mountains above Bø, in a valley between two mountain tops. There, by the lake, you are in raw nature, with no trace of civilisation, except for a small mountain cottage located there. No sounds from driving cars, no light pollution in the evening, and no village are visible from the site.

**How to get there:**

When you drive from Sørvágur towards Bø, there is a large river, Breiðá, halfway between the two villages. If you follow river Breiðá all the way up, you get to the heart-shaped lake high up in the mountains.

It is a steep climb to get up there, and the climb is estimated to take an hour. Even though the climb is steep, it is considered a safe hike.

## The Guardian on Blue Mountain

Blábjørg, or Blue Mountain, is named for its blue tones when the weather is warm during the summer. The mountain is far away enough from Fuglafjørður that the warm summer air is seen colouring the dramatic mountain high above Fuglafjørður.

Blábjørg has a gorge called Mansgjógv, or the Man's Gorge. It has its name from the stone pillar that stands in it, which from the village resembles a man. Some call him the guardian of Fuglafjørður.

## How to get there:

A climb up to Blue Mountain and the Man in the Gorge is a moderately strenuous hike from Fuglafjørður. You can start your hike by walking up the valley west of the village, known as *Vesturi í Dal*. Start your hike from the waterfall, and follow the river up the valley, where you'll see the Blue Mountain in front of you to your right. Continue through the valley all the way up to the mountain pass to the left of Blue Mountain. When you've reached that point, turn right, continuing behind the mountain ridge. That way, you'll reach the Man, a very scenic and picturesque place. If you wish to climb the mountain top itself, you should head directly up to it when you reach the mountain pass above the valley.

## The Hidden River of Kluftá

One of the most iconic areas in the Faroese nature is up in the river Kluftá. Many enjoyable natural areas are hidden by this river, even though it is close to the village and cannot be seen down from the village.

If you decide to go, please do not swim in the river since it is the drinking water of Vík, the village below.

**How to get there:**

When you're in the village Vík, park your car and head towards the large stream that flows through the village centre, bypassing the octagonal church.

Follow the river up the mountainside by entering one of the gates in the fences blocking the trail up. By doing this, you'll get there.

## Stakkurin

In the summer, and during sheep herding, people go out in the sea stack, known as Stakkurin, using a telpher line. High above the sea, people sit there in a small open carriage that gets pulled to and from the stack.

One can only get onto the sea stack by hiring a local guide with access to the telpher system. The carriage is locked so that it cannot be used without a key to unlock it.

If you are afraid of heights, this trip is not recommended, and if you aren't usually afraid of heights, this trip might well be too challenging for you. But, if you feel brave enough, it is a fantastic experience you cannot try in other places around the Faroe Islands.

If you wish to go, you can contact the tour guide at stakkurtours@hotmail.com or (+298) **26 63 43**. The trips to the sea stacks are not part of any commercialised tours, and you might have to ask very politely to be able to go.

## Kirkjubøreyn: The Dessert Moon Landscape

In the old village path between Kirkjubø and Tórshavn, there is a large desert area on the top of the mountains. There, you are entirely away from civilisation in a vast rocky area, in a terrain unlike anywhere else on the Faroe Islands.

This place is not part of any tourist attraction, and very few locals ever walk this area.

If you decide to go, **you must notify someone before going**, and **bring a fully charged mobile phone**, as you cannot expect to meet anyone in that part of the mountains.

**How to get there:**

You can get to this area by walking up the mountainside in Kirkjubø, starting by the cattle grid when you enter the village.

## The Water Dams in Vestmanna

Above the village of Vestmanna, several water dams provide a large part of the electricity on the Faroe Islands. The dams are some of the oldest still in-use electricity plants on the islands and are relatively large in size.

## How to get there:

It can be tricky to find the way up since the roads in Vestmanna can be pretty confusing. But, when you arrive at the village, you turn to your first right and then your first right again, and you'll reach the dams. The roads are narrow and in poor shape, but they are driveable.

**Be careful and respect the signs that have been put up. They have been placed there for a very good reason. Not respecting the signs can be dangerous!**

## The Light House on Akraberg and the Frisian colony

South of the village Sumba, you find Akraberg, where there are a few houses and a lighthouse. Here, it is said, that a Frisian colony once lived, which for hundreds of years lived, parallel to the Norse settlers of the Faroe Islands.

In Akraberg, you'll find a phenomenal view, which the light house only adds to. It is a more picturesque scene, perfect for your social media accounts.

Akraberg is easy to drive to, but the road is poor, though driveable.

**How to get there:**

When you're in the village of Sumba, you can see a small narrow road that leads into the mountains. It is recommended to drive on that road, no matter if you intend to go to Akraberg, or if you just want a drive on a scenic route.

When you drive up this road, you'll find a crossroad, where the narrow road also continues to your right. Follow that road all the way out, and you'll get there.

It can be difficult to find this road, so don't hesitate to ask the locals for direction.

## Cleft Rituskorð

In the mountains above Sandvík in Suðuroy, to the west of the village, there is a wooden bridge, high above a deep gorge, that leads all the way down into the sea. If you are afraid of heights, this trip is not recommended. If you, however, are in for a thrilling experience, walking this bridge can do it for you.

It is an easy hike from the village and an estimated walk of 40 minutes.

**Disclaimer: Walking on the bridge is at its own risk, and only one person is allowed at a time!**

If you decide to go, be careful of your surroundings and not go too close to the edge.

**How to get there:**

In Sandvík, you'll see a small road or trail that leads up through the valley, surpassing the river of Sandvíksá. Follow that road all the way up until you see the cliff edges. When you have come up, you can find the bridge on your left-hand side when facing the cliff edge.

## Holið í Helli: The Troll Cave

In Froðba, there is a cave where it is said that a troll woman resides. This cave is by the shore, and when the tide is high, the cave isn't accessible. When the tide is low, you can walk in. The cave is filled with water-rolled stones, which form a rocky beach within it.

If you decide to go, do not take any of the rocky stones with you as these are protected and, therefore, illegal to take from the site.

## How to get there:

When you're in Sumba, drive as far to the east as possible. There you'll find a small parking space and a bench. There, you'll also find a fence with a gate. Walk through it and head north, straight ahead through the gate. There, you'll find it.

## The Most Rural Places Accessible by Car

In the mountains above Vágur, Suðuroy, a narrow road leads beyond the mountains. Following this road, you can visit three distinct places, all among the top three most rural places you can visit by car.

One of these places is the small village of Fámará which only accounts for one farm that has been abandoned for years. The road leading there is rough, and driving there without an SUV **is not advisable**.

The two other places are the village of Botnur, which only accounts for one house and two other power plant buildings, and Lake Ryskivatn, which lies above Botnur, where the power plant gets its water from the water turbines. You can drive to Bornur and Lake Ryskivatn, but the road and the steep mountainsides are rough. Therefore, it is not recommended for anyone who isn't an experienced driver to go there by car. It isn't recommended for anyone afraid of heights, either.

If you wish to visit these places without driving, you can hike there by following a path made for that purpose.

**How to get there:**

Both Botnur and Ryskivatn are accessible by Google Maps; Fámará is not. But if you tap in Botnur or Ryskivatn on Google Maps, you will get to the narrow road leading to all three places. On the road, road signs lead you to all three places, with Fármará road leading in a different direction which you can see by a crossroad.

If you wish to hike, you can find the route by either following the road or the walking trails, which you can find on the information signs in the village of Vágur. The information signs are located in the village centre.

# Exclusive and Authentic High-end Souvenirs

If you wish to bring home something from your stay in the Faroe Islands, nothing is better than buying a souvenir that you'll be happy to have bought as a souvenir and an item you can use. Here are some recommendations which will make you more happy with your bought memories.

## Knitted clothing

If you'd like to purchase a Faroese knitted sweater, traditional or modern, there are a wide number of shops you can go to. In Tórshavn, you'll find **Sirri**, **Shishabrand**, **Einstakt** and **Guðrun & Guðrun**. In Toftir, you can visit **Navia**, which also has a shop in SMS, the shopping centre in Tórshavn. Snældan has a shop in Strendur, but also in Tórshavn. In Klaksvík there's also a shop called **Hjá Vimu**.

Alternatively, you can buy home-knitted sweaters from one of the home craft shops (see page 130).

## Leirlist Ceramics

At Leirlist Ceramics, you can buy handmade Japanese-inspired pottery made from clay infused with sand, iron and other things found in the Faroese mountains. Leirlist Ceramics has a small workshop and shop in a small basement in the heart of Tórshavn, and also, there is a small self-managed shop where you can take what is presented on a wooden shelf by leaving your payment in the mailbox. To make this purchase, you must, of course, have cash.

Address:   Sjúrðargøta 16, Tórshavn
Phone:     (+298) 25 32 51
e-mail:    leirlist@olivant.fo


## Book shops

A book is always a good memory to have, and here you can buy Faroese books written in English, which might otherwise be difficult to find in the rest of the world. If you wish to buy a book, you can do so at the Airport in Vágar, or you can visit some local bookshops, such as Rit & Rák in the shopping centre in Tórshavn, or at Gamli Bókahandil, the old bookstore in the centre of Tórshavn.

**Østrøm**

Østrøm is a shop that focuses on high-end quality crafts from the Faroes. You can get Faroese-made jewellery, pottery, designer clothes, household goods carved from driftwood, etc.

**Fine Art**

Bring a part of Faroese culture with you by buying an authentic Faroese painting at one of the art shops or purchasing an art poster at one of the galleries.

If this idea sounds appealing, a great tip is to visit Steinprent Galleries in Tórshavn, where original lithographs can be bought cheaply. Steinprent is affordable and one of Europe's highest-quality lithographic printing presses presenting contemporary fine art by Faroese and Scandinavian artists.

Another way of buying art is by visiting Myndlist, Glarsmiðjan or Gallarí Havnará. These galleries focus mainly on acrylics- and oil paintings and are more expensive.

If you want something special for the lowest cost, visit the National Museum of Art or the Art Museum in Sandur. Both have art posters and postcards with famous Faroese paintings.

## Beer and Spirits

Though it may not be a lasting memory, you may wish to purchase a sample beer six-pack from one of the local breweries or a bottle of alcohol, such as whisky, gin or vodka, from one of the local distilleries. That way, you can enjoy more of the Faroes and even share your experiences with your friends over a beer or drink.

# How to get around

It can be pretty tricky to get around in the Faroe Islands. Depending on your needs, you should consider whether you'd like to rely on public transportation or you should rent a car. Public transport can take you to most places, though it can be tricky to visit some rural areas. If you wish to see the larger towns, public transportation is a very well-suited way.

If you decide to rent a car, most larger islands have car ferries, which you can take but cannot book in advance. If you choose to bring your vehicle onto a ferry, you should be by the ferry in good time (at least an hour before the scheduled time).

**Public Transportation**

*Strandferðarskip Landsins* is a public transportation company. On their website, schedules for ferries and busses can be found. Cancellations are notified on their website if stormy or misty weather affects any offered routes.

See more: www.ssl.fo/en/

# THE OBSCURE AND FUN FACTS OF THE FAROE ISLANDS

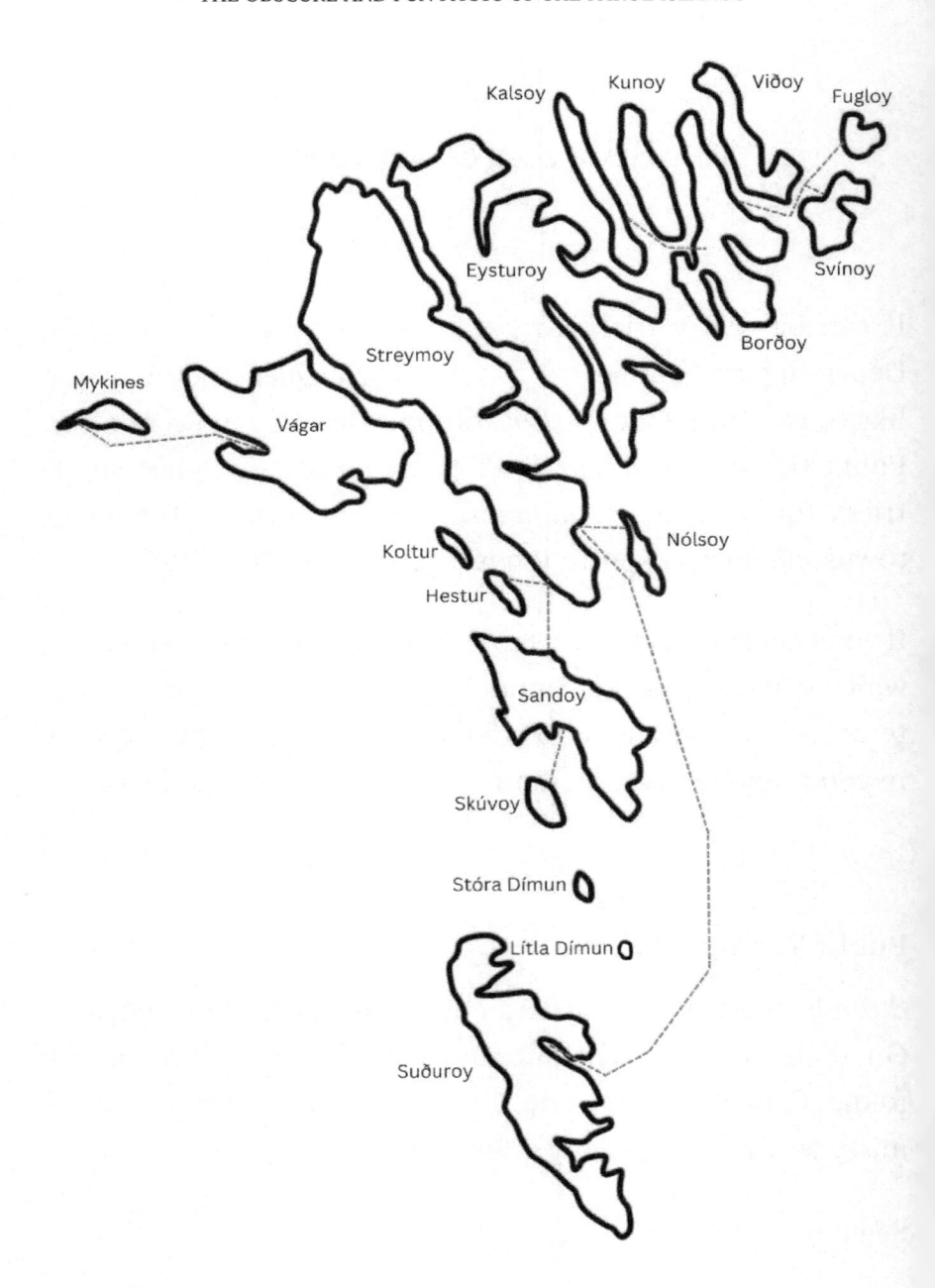

*Sailing routes between the islands*

## Helicopters

The Faroese airline, Atlantic Airways, offers transportation by helicopter to some islands. When the helicopter is in route, you can travel by air for a fairly decent prize, with prizes varying from 255 DKK to 1080 DKK. However, if you wish to travel by helicopter, booking must be made ahead.

The helicopter can also be rented for 35.000 DKK pr. hour, and there are some high-end tours with sightseeing on the island of Vágar and a James Bond tour flown on the island of Kallsoy.

See more: www.atlanticairways.fo/en

THE OBSCURE AND FUN FACTS OF THE FAROE ISLANDS

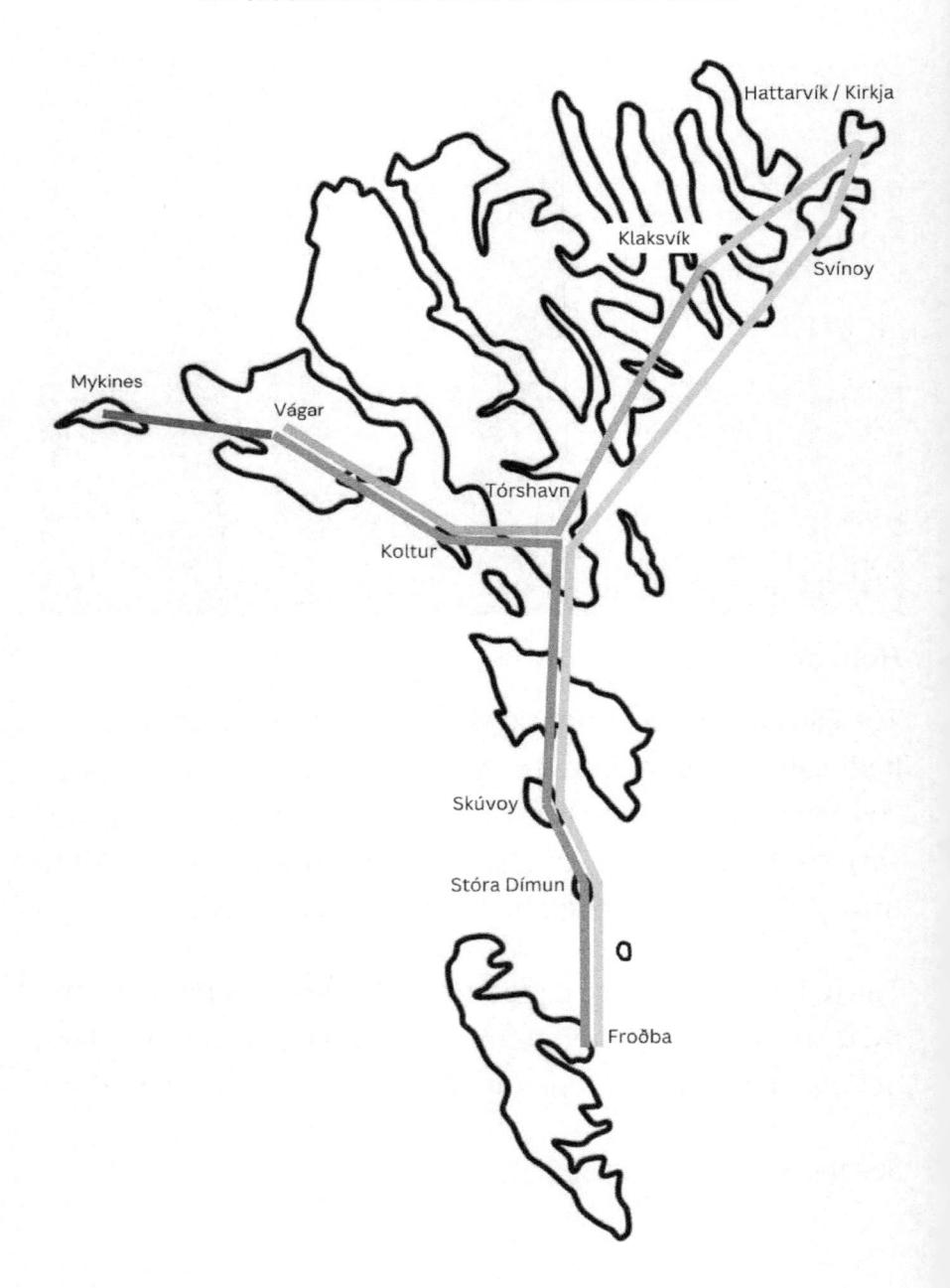

*Helicopter routes between islands and towns*

## Rental cars

Driving your car is the easiest way to get around in the Faroes. It isn't always easy to get around using public transportation, especially if you want to visit some of the rural places. Also, by driving, you can choose some of the more scenic routes, which can only add to your travelling experience. Car rental can be pretty expensive, though.

There are many car rental options. A complete list is available on the website for Vagar Airport.

See more: www.fae.fo

## Toll Roads

All subsea tunnels are toll roads. Therefore, going through the prices before you drive through these tunnels is advised.

## Prices:

*Norðuroyartunnilin*, the subsea tunnel between Eysturoy and Borðoy:

> 100 DKK
> 20 DKK with a tunnel subscription.

*Vágatunnilin*, the subsea tunnel between Streymoy and Vágar:

> 100 DKK
> 20 DKK with a tunnel subscription.

*Eysturoyartunnilin*, the subsea tunnel between Eysturoy and Streymoy:

> 175 DKK
> 75 DKK with a tunnel subscription.

See more: www.tunnil.fo

If you decide to rent a car, **always ask if the rental is with or without a tunnel subscription**. Also, tolls can be paid at the nearby tank stations.

**The Buttercup Routes**

These roads are marked with a buttercup sign, and generally, these roads are more scenic and have lesser traffic than others. But, some of these roads are in rough shape, which is worth considering before you go.

List of Buttercup Routes:

- The Road to Gásadalur (Vágar).
- The Road to Saksun (Streymoy).
- The Road to Múla (Borðoy).
- The Road to Oyndarfjørður (Eysturoy).
- The Road to Elduvík (Eysturoy).
- The Road between Eiði, Funningsfjørður and Gjógv (Eysturoy).
- The Road to Tjørnuvík (Streymoy).
- The Road between Nes, Æðuvík and Runavík (Eysturoy).
- The Mountain Road between Tórshavn and Kollafjørður (Streymoy).
- The Mountain Road between Lopra, Víkarbyrgi and Sumba (Suðuroy).
- The Mountain Road from Øravík to Hov (Suðuroy).

Another unofficial road is the Mountain Road between Leirvík and Fuglafjørður (Eysturoy).

THE OBSCURE AND FUN FACTS OF THE FAROE ISLANDS

# Safety Guidelines for Driving

If you decide to rent a car, here is some need-to-know information crucial for safe driving.

Many more scenic roads are narrow, so you must be extra careful while driving.

- Be careful of sheep roaming the main roads, especially on the smaller, more narrow scenic roads.
- If you drive on narrow roads, remember to use the lay-by for oncoming traffic.
- If you are driving downhill, then make sure to stop for the oncoming traffic that is driving uphill.
- Some tunnels have only one lane. Be careful when driving in those tunnels, and remember to respect the oncoming traffic by using the lay-by.
- The speed limit is 80 kilometres per hour, please do not drive any faster or slower than 80.
- Off-road driving is prohibited by law.
- Do not drink and drive.
- Remember to turn on the headlights.
- Remember to fasten your seatbelts.
- Talking on a handheld telephone is prohibited by law.
- Drive safely.

# THE OBSCURE AND FUN FACTS OF THE FAROE ISLANDS

# Safety Guidelines for Hiking

If you decide to travel to the Faroe Islands, here is some need-to-know information which will be crucial for your trip.

**Clothing**

The weather in the Faroe Islands is almost always wet and cold. Even in the summer, when the weather can be good, it is not guaranteed to stay that way. Therefore, it is essential that you bring warm and waterproof clothing if you plan to go – especially if part of your trip is planned out in nature.

If you're hiking, don't wear slippery clothes, as it can be very dangerous to slip on the steep mountainsides. Also, remember always to wear proper hiking shoes.

**Hiking**

It is legal to hike in most places in the mountains. But however, there are some restricted areas and some seasons which make the trips either illegal or not advisable. If you plan to hike, always remember to ask or notify the local tourist information office. In the chapter, Important Phone Numbers, you can find the phone number of the local tourist information office.

If you decide to go on a hike, then please follow the following instructions:

- Never hike alone. When or if possible, you should hire a local guide.
- Never hike in foggy weather.
- Never hike in pouring rain or during a storm.
- Always check the weather forecast before leaving. The weather can change quicker than you can imagine.
- Keep away from cliff edges.
- Respect fences and signs that are put up for tourists and hikers.
- Investigate seasonal farming and hunting activities.
- Never wear slippery clothes or shoes when hiking.
- Remember to wear warm and waterproof clothing.
- Hiking boots are recommended.
- If you plan on taking a long hike, remember to eat before you go, and preferably bring something edible and drinkable with you.
- Litter is disposed of in trash bins. Bring the litter with you until you return home if you can't find one.
- Make sure always to inform someone before you go on a hike. If you don't know anyone, contact the local tourist information centre before you go.
- Remember to bring a fully charged phone with you.

Do not hike during the hare hunting season, which is from 2nd November to 31st of December.

Sheep herding activities are in the spring and fall. If you see people herding sheep, keep away.

# Important Websites

Visit Faroe Islands:         www.visitfaroeislands.fo

Guide to Faroe Islands:      www.guidetofaroeislands.fo

Public Transportation:       www.ssl.fo

Atlantic Airways:            www.ssl.fo

Take-away:                   www.menu.fo

Online phone book:           www.sona.fo

The Official Site of the Faroe Islands: www.faroeislands.fo

# THE OBSCURE AND FUN FACTS OF THE FAROE ISLANDS

# Important Phone Numbers

## Emergency calls

- Emergency Calls:     112
- Police Station:      114
- Doctor:              118

## Taxi Companies

- Taxi Bil             (+298) 32 32 32
- Mini Buss Taxa       (+298) 21 21 21
- Taxa Snar            (+298) 77 77 78
- Auto                 (+298) 36 36 36

## Hotels

- Hotel Føroyar            (+298) 31 75 00
- Hotel Hafnia             (+298) 31 32 33
- Hotel Tórshavn           (+298) 35 00 00
- Hotel Brandan            (+298) 30 92 00
- Hilton Garden Inn        (+298) 41 40 00
- Hotel Djurhuus           (+298) 35 55 00
- Havgrím Seaside Hotel    (+298) 20 14 00
- 62N Hotel                (+298) 50 06 00
- Hotel Runavík            (+298) 66 33 33

- Hotel Klaksvík         (+298) 45 53 33
- Hotel Norð             (+298) 45 12 44
- Hotel Tvøroyri         (+298) 37 11 71
- Hotel Bakkin           (+298) 25 04 44
- Gamla Hotellið Magenta (+298) 28 64 08
- Giljanes Hostel        (+298) 33 34 65

**Camping**

- Vágur Camping          (+298) 23 93 90
- Trongisvágur Camping   (+298) 61 10 80
- Fámjin Camping         (+298) 37 20 46
- Hvalba Camping         (+298) 23 75 65
- Dalur Camping          (+298) 21 79 01
- Sandur Camping         (+298) 22 20 78
- Giljanes Camping       (+298) 33 34 65
- Mykines Camping        (+298) 21 29 85
- Tórshavn Camping       (+298) 30 24 25
- Vestmanna Camping      (+298) 21 22 45
- Lómundaroyri Camping   (+298) 42 40 01
- Víkar Camping          (+298) 28 61 99
- Eiði Camping           (+298) 21 93 77
- Fuglafjørður Camping   (+298) 23 80 15
- Elduvík Camping        (+298) 41 70 60
- Gjógv Camping          (+298) 42 31 71
- Æðuvík Camping         (+298) 22 17 68
- Svínoy Camping         (+298) 45 69 39
- Mikladalur Camping     (+298) 45 69 39

**Tourist Information Centres**

- Visit Faroe Islands  (+298) 66 65 55
- Visit Suðuroy  (+298) 61 10 80 and (+298) 23 93 90
- Visit Sandoy  (+298) 22 20 78 and (+298) 72 01 00
- Visit Vágar  (+298) 33 34 55
- Visit Tórshavn  (+298) 30 24 25
- Visit Nólsoy  (+298) 52 70 60
- Visit Eysturoy  (+298) 23 80 15 and (+298) 41 70 60
- Visit Norðoy  (+298) 45 69 39

Printed in Great Britain
by Amazon